# WHAT SHALL WE DO

# WITH OUR DAUGHTERS?

## SUPERFLUOUS WOMEN

### AND OTHER LECTURES

BY

MARY A. LIVERMORE

**WILDSIDE PRESS**

## PREFACE.

THE substance of this book has been before the public for more than a decade in the form of lyceum lectures, delivered hundreds of times to audiences in all sections of the country from Maine to California. Three of them are given in the first six chapters of the book; a different arrangement being observed from that followed in the public lectures, not only to avoid repetition, but for a more orderly presentation of the subject. Two, on nearly related topics, are given in the last chapter, with some omissions, and yet with more elaboration.

I have endeavored to eliminate from these printed lectures the peculiarities of platform speech, hoping to make a more readable book. And while I cannot expect that it will be received with the favor shown the lectures, when the novelty of the topics gave them a large hearing, I yet hope the predictions of those who are responsible for their publication may be realized, and that the printed page may find readers where lecturers are rarely heard. For, however imperfectly I may have treated them, the subjects discussed in these pages are of vast importance, and concern directly one-half the human race, and indirectly the whole humanity. Painfully conscious of defects of method and expression, I trust that my life-long interest in all that relates to women, and my honest desire to aid in the great movements that seek their advancement, may disarm criticism, and win favor for this volume, with those who are intrusted with the education of girls.

MARY A. LIVERMORE.

MELROSE, MASS., September, 1883.

# CONTENTS.

| CHAPTER | PAGE |
|---|---|
| I. CHANGED CONDITIONS OF WOMAN'S LIFE | 7 |
| II. PHYSICAL EDUCATION | 20 |
| III. HIGHER EDUCATION | 43 |
| IV. NEED OF PRACTICAL TRAINING | 59 |
| V. INDUSTRIAL AND TECHNICAL TRAINING | 82 |
| VI. MORAL AND RELIGIOUS TRAINING | 119 |
| VII. SUPERFLUOUS WOMEN | 132 |
|     CAUSES OF A SURPLUS OF WOMEN | 144 |
|     NOT A NEW FEATURE OF CIVILIZATION | 153 |
|     CELIBACY NOT ORIGINAL WITH THE CATHOLIC CHURCH | 160 |
|     MARRIAGE NOT THE ONLY BUSINESS OF WOMEN | 165 |
|     CATHOLIC "SUPERFLUOUS WOMEN" | 169 |
|     PROTESTANT "SUPERFLUOUS WOMEN" | 181 |
|     WHO ARE "SUPERFLUOUS WOMEN"? | 202 |
|     RELATION OF MAN AND WOMAN | 205 |

# WHAT SHALL WE DO WITH OUR DAUGHTERS?

## CHAPTER I.

### CHANGED CONDITIONS OF WOMAN'S LIFE.

NEARLY forty years ago, Margaret Fuller, standing, as she said, "in the sunny noon of life," wrote a little book, which she launched on the current of thought and society. It was entitled "Woman in the Nineteenth Century;" and as the truths it proclaimed, and the reforms it advocated, were far in advance of public acceptance, its appearance was the signal for an immediate, widespread, newspaper controversy, that raged with great violence. I was young then; and as I took the book from the hands of the bookseller, wondering what the contents of the thin little volume could be, to provoke so wordy a strife, I opened at the first page. My attention was immediately arrested, and a train of thought started, by the two mottoes at the head of the opening chapter, — one underneath the other, one contradicting the other.

The first was an old-time adage, indorsed by Shakspeare, believed in by the world, and quoted in that day very generally. It is not yet entirely obsolete. "Frailty, thy name is Woman." Underneath it, and unlike it was the other, — "The Earth waits for her Queen." The first described woman as she has been understood in the past; as she has masqueraded in history; as she has been made to figure in literature; as she has, in a certain sense, existed. The other prophesied of that grander type of woman, towards which to-day the whole sex is moving, — consciously or unconsciously, willingly or unwillingly, — because the current sets that way, and there is no escape from it.

No one who has studied history, even superficially, will for a moment dispute the statement, that, during the years of which we have had historic account, there has brooded very steadily over the female half of the human family an air of repression, of limitation, of hindrance, of disability, of gloom, of servitude. If there have been epochs during which women have been re-

garded equal to men, they have been brief and
abnormal. Among the Hindoos, woman was the
slave of man, forbidden to speak the language of
her master, and compelled to use the *patois* of
slaves. The Hebrews pronounced her an after-
thought of the Deity, and the mother of all evil.
The Greek law regarded her as a child, and held
her in life-long tutelage. The Greek philoso-
phers proclaimed her a "monster," "an accidental production." Mediæval councils declared her
unfit for instruction. The early Christian fathers
denounced her as a " noxious animal," a " painted
temptress," a "necessary evil," a "desirable
calamity," a "domestic peril." From the English
Heptarchy to the Reformation the law proclaimed the wife to be " in all cases, and under
all circumstances, her husband's creature, servant,
slave." To Diderot, the French philosopher,
even in the eighteenth century, she was only a
"courtesan;" to Montesquieu, an "attractive
child;" to Rousseau, "an object of pleasure
to man." To Michelet, nearly a century later,
she was a "natural invalid." Mme. de Staël
wrote truly, "that, of all the faculties with which
Nature had gifted woman, she had been able to
exercise fully but one, — the faculty of suffering."

The contemptuous opinion entertained of woman in the past has found expression, not alone in literature, but also in unjust laws and customs. "In marriage she has been a serf; as a mother she has been robbed of her children; in public instruction she has been ignored; in labor she has been a menial, and then inadequately compensated; civilly she has been a minor, and politically she has had no existence. She has been the equal of man only when punishment, and the payment of taxes, were in question."

Born and bred for generations under such conditions of hindrance, it has not been possible for women to rise much above the arbitrary standards of inferiority persistently set before them. Here and there through the ages some woman endowed with phenomenal force of character has towered above the mediocrity of her sex, hinting at the qualities imprisoned in the feminine nature. It is not strange that these instances have been rare: it is strange, indeed, that women have held their own during these ages of degradation. And as, by a general law of heredity, " the inheritance of traits of character is persistent in proportion to the length of time they have been inherited," it is easy to account for the conservatism of

## Changed Conditions of Woman's Life. 11

women to-day, and for the indifference, not to say hostility, with which many regard the movements for their advancement.

For humanity has moved forward to an era where wrong and slavery are being displaced, and reason and justice are being recognized as the rule of life. Science is extending immeasurably the bounds of knowledge and power; art is refining life, giving to it beauty and grace; literature bears in her hands whole ages of comfort and sympathy; industry, aided by the hundred-handed elements of nature, is increasing the world's wealth; and invention is economizing its labor. The age looks steadily to the redressing of wrong, to the righting of every form of error and injustice; and a tireless and prying philanthropy, which is almost omniscient, is one of the most hopeful characteristics of the time.

If the barbaric spirit of war still lingers among the nations, so also does the voice of Charles Sumner, who for thirty years taught that "the true grandeur of nations is peace." If slavery fastens fetters on the bodies and souls of human beings, Garrison and Phillips cry aloud for immediate emancipation: the nation joins in the holy crusade for liberty, and slavery dies. If the cry of the criminal comes up from prisons noisome with filth, and foul with moral pollution, the tendency of the age is, not only to realize the ideal of Howard, that "prisons should be made moral reformatories," but to organize societies for the prevention of crime. If ignorance cowers in darkness in sections of the land, a plea is made for universal, compulsory education, on the tenable ground that a republic cannot live with an illiterate constituency behind it.

Indeed the world has travelled so far on the line of humanity, that, when disaster overtakes cities and nations, it virtually forgets its ancient sectional and national divisions. America has again and again sent food to Ireland when famine was stalking among her people gaunt and hollow. The North has despatched swift relief to the South when it was smitten with pestilence; the East has been moved to unstinted beneficence when the West has been devastated by floods and hurricanes; and when Chicago was consumed by a conflagration that raged seven miles along the lake-shore, and burned the homes of a hundred thousand people, who encamped on the shelterless prairie, the whole world felt the calamity like a personal woe. It subsidized the swift speech of the lightning in which to proffer help, and for forty-eight hours the earth rolled in its orbit, belted with telegrams alive and glowing with divinest sympathy and helpfulness. So royally did the states and nations of the world keep their promises, that after Chicago had helped all in need of assistance, and there was no longer an applicant for relief within her limits, she had yet a million and a half of dollars in bank for which she had no immediate need; and she bestowed it on her charitable institutions. Notwithstanding deplorable corruption in politics, dishonesty in business, and immorality in social life, there is so tender and humane a spirit dominating the age in which we live, that even the brute creation share in it, and we have hundreds of societies organized to prevent cruelty to animals.

It could not be possible in such an era but that women should share in the justice and kindliness with which the time is fraught. A great wave is lifting them to higher levels. The leadership of the world is being taken from the hands of the brutal and low, and the race is groping its way to a higher ideal than once it knew. It is the evolution of this tendency that is lifting women out of their subject condition, that is emancipating them from the seclusion of the past, and adding to the sum total of the world's worth and wisdom, by giving to them the cultivation human beings need. The demand for their education, — technical and industrial, as well as intellectual, — and for their civil and political rights, is being urged each year by an increasing host, and with more emphatic utterance.

The doors of colleges, professional schools, and universities, closed against them for ages, are opening to them. They are invited to pursue the same courses of study as their brothers, and are graduated with the same diplomas. Trades, businesses, remunerative vocations, and learned professions seek them; and even the laws, which are the last to feel the change in public opinion, — usually dragging a whole generation behind, — even these are being annually revised and amended, and then they fail to keep abreast of the advancing civilization.

All this is but prefatory, and prophetic of the time when, for women, law will be synonymous with justice, and no opportunity for knowledge or effort will be denied them on the score of sex.

As I listen to the debates that attend this progress, and weigh the prophecies of evil always inspired by a growing reform; as I hear the clash of the scientific raid upon women, by the small pseudo-scientists of the day, — who make of "The Popular Science Monthly" and "The North-American Review" catapults for the hurling of their missiles, — my thoughts turn to the young women of the present time. "What shall we do with our daughters?" is really the sum and substance of what, in popular phrase, is called "the woman question." For if to-morrow all should be done that is demanded by the wisest reformer, and the truest friend of woman, it would not materially affect the condition of the adult women of society. Their positions are taken, their futures are forecast; and they are harnessed into the places they occupy, not unfrequently, by invisible, but omnipotent, ties of love or duty. Obedience to the behests of duty gives peace, even when love is lacking; and peace is a diviner thing than happiness.

It is for our young women that the great changes of the time promise the most: it is for our daughters, — the fair, bright girls, who are the charm of society and the delight of home; the sources of infinite comfort to fathers and mothers, and the sources of great anxiety also. What shall we do with them, — and what shall they do with and for themselves?

> "New occasions teach new duties,
> Time makes ancient good uncouth," —

and the training of fifty years ago is not sufficient for the girls of to-day. The changed conditions of life which our young women confront compel greater care and thought on the part of those charged with their education than has heretofore been deemed necessary. They are to be weighted with larger duties, and to assume heavier responsibilities; for the days of tutelage seem to be ended for civilized women, and they are to think and act for themselves.

Let no one, therefore, say this question of the training of our daughters is a small question. No question can be small that relates to half the human race. The training of boys is not more important than that of girls. The hope of many is so centred in the "coming man," that the only questions of interest to them are those propounded by James Parton in "The Atlantic Monthly," — "Will the coming man smoke?" "Will he drink wine?" and so on to the end of the catechism. But let it not be forgotten, that, before this "coming man" will make his appearance, his mother will precede him, and that he will be very largely what his mother will make him. Men are to-day confessing their need of the aid of women by appointing them on school committees, boards of charities, as prison commissioners, physicians to insane-asylums, — positions which they cannot worthily fill without preparation.

Nor let us forget the vast influence exerted by women upon men, sometimes worthily, and sometimes, alas! disastrously. We often see a man starting in life, lacking largeness of aim and fineness of organization. Left to himself he would drift on the current of society wherever it might bear him. But a kind fate harnesses him, in love or friendship, with a woman of nobler character. Seeing farther than the narrow present, and deeper than the gilded surface, she transfuses him with her own spirit, inspires him with noble purposes, and he becomes a power for good. Only yesterday this newspaper paragraph caught my eye: —

"Mrs. ——, who has found consolation since her husband's death in continuing the charities which he had begun, has just given ten thousand dollars to the Old

### 18  *What shall we do with our Daughters?*

Ladies' Home, and five thousand dollars to the Humane Society."

But it was the wife who "*began* the charities." When vast wealth came suddenly to this couple the husband would have spent it in coarse pleasures. But she won him to deeds of helpfulness, an interest in the unfortunate, a generous friendliness toward all; and to "bear the burdens of others" gradually became the grand passion of his life. Dying childless, he bequeathed her all his property without restrictions or directions, saying, "She knows better than I what to do with it."

And have we not all known men of rare promise, whose early manhood has glowed with high ambitions, but who, alas! have been made petty, ill-natured, and ignoble by their female companions? These, through physical weakness, mental poverty, and lowness of moral tone, have shut down, like brakes, on the progress of husbands, sons, and brothers, halting them, lowering their ideals, till at last their very manhood has died out, and their faces have become tombstones, written all over with obituaries of dead souls within.

Therefore, not only for their own sakes, but for

## Changed Conditions of Woman's Life. 19

the sake of the human family, of which women make one-half, should we look carefully to the training of our daughters. Nature has so constituted us, that the sexes act and re-act upon each other, making every "woman's cause" a man's cause, and every man's cause a woman's cause; so that we
"Rise or sink
Together, dwarfed or godlike, bond or free."

And they are the foes of the race, albeit not intentional, who set themselves against the removal of woman's disabilities, shut in their faces the doors of education or opportunity, or deny them any but the smallest and most incomplete training. For it is true that "who educates a woman, educates a race."

## CHAPTER II.

#### PHYSICAL EDUCATION.

Good health is a great pre-requisite of successful or happy living. To live worthily or happily, to accomplish much for one's self or others when suffering from pain and disease, is attended with difficulty. Dr. Johnson used to say that "every man is a rascal when he is sick." And very much of the peevishness, irritability, capriciousness, and impatience seen in men and women has its root in bodily illness. The very morals suffer from disease of the body. Therefore I would give to "our daughters" a good physical education.

"But suppose my daughter is so unfortunate as to have a sickly body at birth?"

Learn what is the cause of her feebleness, what is the defect in her physical organization, and then how to remedy it by wise, hygienic living. Correct living and intelligent physical training will eliminate many of the tendencies to ill health which we bring into the world with us.

We shall by and by come to recognize the right of every child to be well born, — sound in body, with inherited tendencies towards mental and moral health. We have learned that it is possible to direct the operations of nature so as to have finer breeds of horses, cattle, and fowls, to improve our fruits, flowers, and grains. Science searches for the pre-natal laws of being, and comes to the aid of all who wish to improve the lower creation. When shall an enlightened public sentiment demand that those who seek of God the gift of little children shall make themselves worthy the gift by healthful and noble living, practical acquaintance with pre-natal laws of being, and all that relates to the hereditary transmission of qualities?

Canon Kingsley, in his book on "Health and Education," says, "Let duly educated and legally qualified women teach to women what every woman ought to know." "Let woman be restored to her natural share in the sacred office of healer, which she held in the middle ages, and from which she was thrust out during the sixteenth century." During the last decade duly qualified medical women, through books, lectures, and papers, have poured in a flood of light on the subject of the physical education of girls. Drs. Elizabeth Blackwell, Mary Putnam Jacobi, Mary Safford, Sarah Hackett Stevenson, Caroline Hastings, and many others — all thoroughly educated and "duly qualified" women physicians — have put their knowledge of physiology, anatomy, and hygiene at the service of women most generously. By printed and oral speech they have sought to change the conditions and habits of women, which at one time threatened to make womanhood and invalidism interchangeable terms. They have awakened thought, stimulated inquiry, and set in motion a reform that was needed.

Other books have been written by men physicians, some of them valuable, and others so technical as not to be adapted to popular use. Some of these works, written by specialists, are calculated to do injury. One would suppose in reading them that women possessed but one class of physical organs, and that these are always diseased. Such teaching is pestiferous, and tends to cause and perpetuate the very evils it professes to remedy.

There has been great improvement in the physical habits of women and girls within my memory. In my girlhood girls wore low-necked dresses and

## Physical Education. 23

short sleeves almost universally, except in winter. Many even were thus insufficiently clad in the severest weather. Flannel underwear was unknown, so were rubber shoes and waterproof cloaks. Slippers and thin-soled shoes were worn on the streets in inclement seasons. Very little attention was given to regular bathing, ventilation, or the preparation of healthful food. Instead of mattresses we slept on feathers, and lived in rooms with open fires, which roasted you on one side while you were freezing on the other. Glorified as these same open fires are to-day, I remember them with a shudder. Better houses, better food, more comfort, a more cheerful system of religion, a larger intellectual culture, a nobler outlook for womanhood, — as far as these have prevailed, they have undoubtedly told favorably on the health of women during the last fifty years.

If, however, we would give to our daughters a good physiological training, we must attend carefully to their dress. The dress of women at the present time is about as damaging to health as it well can be. And many of our girls are made the victims of disease and weakness for life through the evils of the dress they wear from birth. The causes of their invalidism are sought in hard study, co-education, too much exercise, or lack of rest and quiet in certain periods when nature demands it. All the while the medical attendant is silent concerning the "glove-fitting," steel-clasped corset, the heavy, dragging skirts, the bands engirding the body, and the pinching, distorting boot. These will account for much of the feebleness of women and girls; for they exhaust energy, make freedom of movement a painful impossibility, and frequently shipwreck our young daughter before she gets out of port.

We begin very early to injure the health of our girls by means of their dress. Riding over the New-York Central Railroad from Albany to Buffalo in a drawing-room car, I observed a lady occupying one of the compartments with her two little children, — a girl and a boy, accompanied by a nurse. The little boy, rosy and happy, made frequent visits to the saloon of the car, where all welcomed him, for he had a gay temper, and overflowed with good-nature and sociability. As he went back to his sister with an orange, an apple, a picture, a pencil, and bit of paper, she would essay to accompany him on his next excursion among us. We would barely catch a gleam of the child's shining face and delicate raiment, when

## Physical Education. 25

the watchful nurse would swoop down upon her, and bear her back within the close, stuffy compartment. What was the matter?

The little boy was sensibly dressed in dark stuff, suitable for travelling, with a white collar about the neck. But his sister wore an immaculate white Marseilles dress, then the fashion for children, ruffled, tucked, shirred, embroidered, and be-furbelowed generally. The dress was tied back with a pink sash of most delicate shade. Her lisle-thread stockings, reaching above the knee, were of the same delicate hue. Her dainty boots were of very light kid. Her hair, soft and shining, like spun gold, was braided and curled, and tied back with ribbons of the same exquisite pink. She wore pink shoulder-knots, held in place by little pins of gold, and was farther adorned with bracelets, finger-rings, and a gold neck-chain with a locket attached. This was the remonstrance made to this over-dressed little creature: "You'll spoil your dress out there, and ruin your pretty stockings, and get your hair all out of curl. You know you want to look nice when you get to auntie's: so you must sit here, and be a lady."

Now, before that ride was ended, the child had

learned a lesson which she will never forget, — that clothes are of small moment to boys, while to girls they are of vast importance, so that enjoyment, comfort, and play must be subordinated to them. This "gospel of good clothes" is continually dinned into the ears of the girl, as she is growing to young womanhood, till she is dominated by it. Is she invited to a picnic, excursion, lawn-party, wedding, or funeral? The first question asked is, "What shall I wear?" Not so with her brother. He knows what he will wear, — the suit out of which he jumped on Sunday night as he bounced into bed, and which, for aught he knows, lies where he doffed it. He will wear that, for he has no other, and he wants no other.

Years roll away, and the little girl reaches womanhood. She has promised her hand to the one man whom she has learned to love. Parents and friends approve of the lover; and she begins her preparations for the future home, which her imagination invests with every charm. In what do these preparations consist? In the manufacture of clothing of every conceivable fashion, to be worn on every supposable occasion, in quantities that are absolutely wasteful. She will sew to the very verge of exhaustion, and go to her new home

## Physical Education. 27

with trunks packed with every thing to wear of which you have ever heard, as well as with garments of whose existence you have never dreamed.

And, if you did not know to the contrary, you might infer that a partnership in marriage includes a partnership in business, and that the newly wedded pair proposed to open a store for the sale of ready-made clothing for women; or that it is the custom of the country for the bride to provide herself with all the clothing needed during her life, the husband being expected to furnish her only such garments as may be necessary at death, — a shroud or grave-gown.

We do even worse than this; for we have a theory, generally accepted in civilized society, which we never formulate in speech, but to which we are very loyal in practical life. This theory, put in plain language, is this: "God knows how to make boys; and when he sends a boy into the world it is safe to allow him to grow to manhood as God has made him. He may be too tall or too short, too stout or too thin, too light or too dark. Nevertheless, it is right, for God understands how to make boys. But when God sends a girl into the world it is not safe to allow her to grow to womanhood as he has made her. Some one must take her, and improve her figure, and give her the shape in which it is proper for her to grow."

Accordingly, our young daughter comes some day from the dressmaker with this demand: "Mme. —— [the dressmaker] says I am getting into horrid shape, and that I must have a pair of corsets immediately." The corsets are bought, and worn, and very soon the physical deterioration begins.

"It does not require the foresight of a seer," says Dr. Mary Safford, "to diagnose a chronic case of tight lacing and of heavy skirts. You know that when the abdominal muscular walls become inert, almost wasted, one of the most important daily functions of the body is rarely, if ever, normally carried on. We might enumerate the ill results that follow; but these are only links in the long chain of disorders that have won the disgraceful appellation of 'women's diseases,' when they should be termed 'women's follies.'"

"Medical students have learned to call the livers of the female subjects that go to the dissecting-room the 'corset-liver,'" says Dr. Mary Studley. "It is the rule, rather than the exception, for these livers to be so deeply indented where the ribs have been crowded against them by im-

## Physical Education. 29

properly worn clothing, that the wrist may be easily laid in the groove. And this is an organ which is a mass of blood-vessels, through which every particle of blood ought to circulate freely on its way to the heart. Of course it cannot get through the squeezed portions; and the inevitable result of the half-done work of the liver is an unclean condition of the blood, which utters its cry by means of aching nerves."

"The Greeks," says Canon Kingsley, "whose figures remain everlasting and unapproachable models of human beauty, wore no stays (corsets). The first mention of stays that I have ever found," he continues, "is in the letters of Synesius, Bishop of Cyrene, on the Greek coast of Africa, about 400 A.D. He tells us how, when he was shipwrecked on a remote part of the coast, and he and the rest of the passengers were starving on cockles and limpets, there was among them a slave girl, out of the far East, who had a pinched wasp-waist; such as you may see on the old Hindoo sculptures, and such as you may see on any street in any British town. And, when the Greek ladies of the neighborhood found her out, they sent for her from house to house, to behold, with astonishment and laughter, this new and prodigious waist, with which it seemed to them impossible for a human being to breathe or live."

He goes on to tell us, this plain-speaking Canon Kingsley, that "in future years, when mankind has learned to obey more strictly those laws of nature and science, which are the will of God, the present fashion of tight lacing will be looked back upon as a contemptible and barbarous superstition, denoting a very low level of civilization in the people which have practised it."

If an artist with a commission to cut in immortal marble a statue of the Goddess of Liberty, of Justice or Peace, an Aurora, the Muses, or Graces, should copy the figure of the fashionable woman made over by the *modiste* and the corsets, he would lose caste, not alone with artists, but with the civilized world. His statue would be received everywhere with laughter and derision. He would seek, instead, as a model, one of the matchless living forms on which no corset has begun its deforming work, and then add another to "those glorious statues which we pretend to admire, but refuse to imitate."

While it is undoubtedly true that the practice of tight lacing is regarded with growing disfavor to-day, it is also true that the corsets in vogue at

## Physical Education. 31

present are more objectionable than those worn even half a century ago. For those were home-made, and while they could be very tightly laced, did not fit the figure well, were free from the torture of whalebones and steel front pieces, all stitched in; while broad straps passing over the shoulders supported them, and the clothing hung upon them. But the modern corset is so ingeniously woven that it presses in upon the body, the muscular walls, the floating ribs, the stomach, the hips, and the abdomen, compelling them to take the form the corset-maker has devised in lieu of that God has given. Stiff whalebones behind, and finely "tempered steel-fronts" pressing into the stomach and curving over the abdomen, keep the figure of the girl erect and unbending, while Nature has made the spine supple with joints.

Physicians have persistently condemned the corset for half a century, even when it was not so harmful an article of dress as it is to-day. The educated medical women, who are gaining in numbers, influence, and practice, denounce it unqualifiedly, lay to its charge no small amount of the dire diseases on whose treatment gynæcologists fatten, and declare that it enhances the perils of maternity, and inflicts upon the world inferior children. Men condemn corsets in the abstract, and sometimes are brave enough to insist that the women of their households shall be emancipated from them ; and yet their eyes have been so generally educated to the approval of the small waist and the hour-glass figure, that they often hinder women who seek a hygienic style of dress.

"Jenny," said a grown-up brother, a man in business, to his youngest sister, a bright, sensible girl in her third college year, "why don't you dress as other girls do?"

"Do I not?" was her surprised reply, as she glanced over her faultless attire, made in the reigning fashion, only handsomer and simpler. "Wherein does my dress differ from that of other girls?"

"Your waist is larger, and your skirts don't bunch out behind as theirs do. I think their style is the prettier."

"Oh," replied his sister, "I wear an emancipation waist, instead of corsets, and I dispense with a bustle."

"Well, I would wear both if I were in your place," was the masculine advice. "I wouldn't cultivate oddity of dress just because I was in college."

"My dress isn't odd: it is like that of other girls," remonstrated the sister. "But as to the corsets and bustle, I cannot wear them: they are not comfortable."

"Oh, that's nonsense!" was the last word of the brother. "Other girls wear them, and you can if you try."

No young, growing girl should be allowed to wear corsets. Instead, let her be fitted with a basque waist, cut to fit the figure; and on the bottom of this waist sew buttons, to hold what skirts she may wear. In the bands of these skirts work buttonholes to correspond with the buttons on the basque; and the wearer will then have plenty of room for heart, stomach, and lungs, while the weight of the skirts will be lifted from the hips, and be borne on the shoulders. Mothers can make this garment for themselves and for their daughters, or it can be easily managed by a dressmaker.

It is a mistake on the part of our daughter that the corset will give her beauty of figure. The young American girl is usually lithe and slender, and requires no artificial intensifying of her slightness. The corset will give her only stiffness of appearance, and interferes with that grace of motion which is one of the charms of young girls.

The basque under-waist, made as a substitute for the corset, and beginning to supersede it, fits the figure trimly, revealing its graceful contour, and is kept in place, — not by bones, or slips of steel, or thickly stitched-in stiff cords, — but by the weight of the skirts buttoned on the lower part. Over this under-waist the outer dress can be fitted; and its waist will be smooth and unwrinkled, — a desideratum to most women.

The stout woman who wears a corset to diminish her proportions only distorts her figure; for her pinched waist causes her broad shoulders and hips to look broader by contrast, while the pressure upon the heart and blood-vessels gives to her face that permanent blowzy flush that suggests apoplexy. "Who can forgive the unhealthy cheek and red nose induced by such a practice?" says Mrs. Haweis in her "Art of Beauty." "And who can forget the disease which has come or is coming?"

If it were certain that the present fashion of short skirts for the street had come in as a permanency, we might all "thank God!" and take courage." But a dreadful fear perpetually haunts one, that there may be a revival of the old-time uncleanness, when women will again drag trailing skirts over country roads, and sweep them through dirty city streets. What would be the criticisms of women, if men — whom we regard as less fastidious than ourselves concerning personal cleanliness and neatness of attire — should follow a corresponding fashion, condemning them to wear their coat-skirts and trousers' legs indefinitely prolonged behind them, till they trailed a half-yard or more, upon the sidewalks? And what, if, to release the hand from the wild clutch of entangling and bedraggled skirts, they should wear at the side a minimized pair of tongs, into whose grasp the vile dragging things might be thrust, and which would then bag about the ankles, flapping with every step? Could men make of themselves a more grotesque spectacle? And do women ever present a more ludicrous sight, than when similarly hampered?

There is yet one other part of the girl's dress to which mothers must give attention.

John Burroughs, in his "Winter Sunshine," expresses the fear that "the American is becoming disqualified for the manly art of walking by a falling-off in the size of his foot. . . . A small, trim foot," he tells us, "well booted or gaitered, is the national vanity. How we stare at the big feet of foreigners, and wonder what may be the price of leather in those countries, and where all the aristocratic blood is, that these plebeian extremities so predominate!"

Col. Higginson informs us, on the high authority of a fashionable New-York shoemaker, that "women are not so vain of their feet as men. A man who thinks he has a handsome foot," says this unimpeachable witness, "is apt to give us more trouble than any lady among our customers. I have noticed this for twenty years."

The prevailing French boots made for women, and exhibited in the shop-windows, are painfully suggestive. Pointed and elongated, they prophesy cramped and atrophied toes; while the high and narrow heel, that slides down under the instep, throws the whole body into an unnatural position in walking, creating diseases which are difficult of cure. "Show me her boots!" said a physician, called to a young lady suffering from unendurable pain in the back and knee-joints, which extended and engirt her, till, to use her own language, "she was solid pain downwards from the waist." "There's the trouble!" was his sententious comment, as he tossed the fashionable torturing boot from him after examination. We send missionaries to China to teach mothers, among other things, not to cramp and distort the feet of their little daughters. Who will send missionaries to Christianized, civilized America, to teach American mothers the same gospel?

Latterly, I have noticed in the windows of some of the shops on Washington and Tremont Streets, Boston, placards, advertising in large letters, "COMMON-SENSE BOOTS FOR GIRLS!" and "COMMON-SENSE BOOTS FOR SCHOOL WEAR!" Almost square at the toe, with broad, thick soles, more fulness in the upper leather, and low, broad heels, to be worn *under* the heel, they are a great improvement upon the Parisian boots. The young people who wear them declare them to be "vastly comfortable," and a foot well fitted with them pleases the eye with its elegance.

The tendency to follow fashions that deform the body is inexplicable; and yet it is found among all people, the savage as well as the civilized. The Polynesian tattooes his body from head to foot. The Australian wears a plug of bone through the cartilage, which divides the nostrils from each other. Many of the East Indians wear rings in their noses, instead of in their ears. The Malays blacken their teeth.

The Zulus bore holes in their ears, which holes they enlarge enormously by stretching. Tribes of North-American Indians flatten the form of the head, commencing the distortion in infancy. The Chinese bandage the feet of women till they fail to be the organs of support and locomotion, and resemble the hoofs of animals in shape. While civilized European and American women not only deform the feet, pierce the ears for the wearing of rings, but compress the waist, till the vital organs are displaced, and frightful diseases are incurred. "Seest thou not," says Shakspeare, "what a deformed thief this fashion is?"

While the clothing of our daughter should not deform the figure, nor injure the health, it need be neither inelegant nor inartistic. No particular style of dress can be recommended, but each one should choose what is most becoming and appropriate in fashion and material. With sacred regard for the laws of health, and without too large expenditure of time and money, every woman should aim to present an attractive exterior to her friends and the world. So, indeed, should every man; for it is the duty of all human beings to be as beautiful as possible.

What is beauty? It is not a mere matter of

pink-and-white complexion, of abundant tresses of hair, of lustrous eyes, shapely shoulders, and exquisite figure; for you will meet people possessing all these traits of physical beauty, and after the first hour the eye wearies of them. You fail to find any charm in them. A graceful shape of decorated china interests you more. You will meet others lacking all these elements of beauty; and after the first interview you are forever attached to them, as with hooks of steel. They enter your home, and glorify it with an indefinable charm. They seem to be invested with the overflowing sunlight, the perfume of flowers, the singing of birds. The best that is in you comes forth to meet them; and for the time you are translated into a gladness, a nobleness, and a fine courtesy higher than your wont.

Beauty comes from within. To be "upright before God, and downright before man," to be honest, faithful, helpful, patient, and kindly disposed, will give a charm to any face, though it be irregular in feature, or framed in white hair and beard. It is within the province of all to possess beauty of this highest order. "There is no beautifier of complexion or form or behavior," says Emerson, "like the wish to scatter joy, and not pain, around us." Nor should women fail to attire themselves tastefully, to adopt costumes that are harmonious in form and color, to give attention to matters of personal decoration. No woman can afford to ignore the attractions of dress, and a badly dressed young woman is always a disappointment. To be well dressed one must avoid unhealthy, absurd, and grotesque styles. The dress must be appropriate to the time and occasion, adapted to the wearer, and must not seem the result of a too lavish outlay of money or time.

I have spoken at length of dress, because of the physical discomfort and hindrance caused by the prevailing dress of women, and because it is also a prolific source of disease, which becomes chronic and incurable. But food, sleep, exercise, and other matters demand attention, when one is intrusted with the education of girls. American children, unlike those which we see abroad, sit at table with their parents, eat the same food, keep the same late hours, and share with them the excitement of evening guests, evening meetings and lectures, and the dissipation of theatres, operas, balls, and receptions. This is unwise indulgence. Children require simple food, early hours for retiring, and abundance of sleep, as well as freedom from social and religious excitements.

I will not enter into a consideration of these matters, but will refer mothers, and those charged with the training of girls, to the excellent books recently written by women physicians for their guidance. "The Physiology of Woman," by Dr. Sarah Hackett Stevenson, who is connected with the Woman's Medical College of Chicago, is one of these books. Another is entitled "What our Girls ought to know," by Dr. Mary J. Studley. "Dress-Reform," edited by Abba Goold Woolson, contains four lectures, delivered by four women physicians, which are invaluable. "The Education of American Girls," edited by Anna C. Brackett, has had a deservedly wide circulation; and the first paper, by the editor, on "The Culture of the Body," should be in every mother's and teacher's possession.

Signs multiply about us that the women of the future will have healthy and strong physiques. Dress-reform associations are organized in the principal American cities; and agencies established to furnish under-garments, or patterns for them, demanded by common-sense and vigorous health. For it is the under-garments that the dress-reform proposes to change. The outer garments may be safely left to the taste of the individual, who has accepted the principles of the dress-reform in the construction of the under-garments. English women are moving in the same sensible direction; and a "Society to promote Rational Dress for Women" has been formed in London, with Viscountess Harberton as president. A new American association has just been formed of collegiate alumnæ; and in their circular they urge upon women students "to bear constantly in mind the fact that the best intellectual results cannot be obtained without perfect physical health." It recommends all women students to "maintain a constant watch over their own habits as regards sleep, food, exercise, and dress;" and declares that "a failure in sufficient sleep, food, and exercise should be lamented equally as a failure in recitation."

Health is a means to an end. It is an investment for the future. That end is worthy work and noble living. And life has little to offer the young girl who has dropped into physical deterioration, which cuts her off from the activities of the time, and makes existence to her synonymous with endurance.

## CHAPTER III.

### HIGHER EDUCATION.

IT is hardly necessary that any thing should be said in advocacy of the higher intellectual education of our daughters. For "with the successes before us of Wellesley and Vassar and Smith Colleges," says Col. Higginson, "of Michigan, Cornell, and Boston Universities; with the spectacle at Cambridge of young women [in the Harvard Annex] actually reading Plato 'at sight' with Professor Goodwin, it surely seems as if the higher education of women might be considered quite beyond the stage of experiment, and might henceforth be provided for in the same common-sense and matter-of-course way which we provide for the education of young men." The question of woman's collegiate education is practically settled; and we may expect that the next quarter of a century will witness almost as great unwisdom in movements for the higher education of women, as has the past in ignoring the subject altogether.

For the tendency of the time is to multiply women's colleges, while the present collegiate institutions of the country can be made available, for all purposes, for some time to come. If the funds expended in founding new colleges for women, which start only partially equipped for their proposed work, were expended in endowing already existing institutions, their efficiency might be greatly increased, and the opportunities for woman's higher education be immensely enhanced in value. This would compel co-education, for which many of the Eastern colleges are not yet ready. A scholarship has been founded at Amherst, the income of which will be given to a woman when women are admitted to the institution. But that day waits.

And yet co-education wisely managed is almost indispensable to the training of noble men and women; for education in its broadest sense takes account of all the influences that go to form character. It is not wholly intellectual, but is moral and social, and can best be carried forward, under a proper *régime*, where young men and women are educated and trained together. The objections to co-education are made chiefly by Eastern educators, and come almost entirely from Eastern colleges and universities. Concisely stated, they may be summed up as follows:—

1. Girls are deficient in the strength of body and mind necessary for the successful pursuit of the college curriculum marked out for boys: co-education would therefore lower the grade of scholarship.

2. Were girls and boys to study together, flirtations and early marriages would be the inevitable result; the girls would become masculine and unwomanly, and the boys effeminate and unmanly. Co-education would, therefore, lower the standard of morals.

3. The great differences of the sexes establish an imperative need for different systems of education. Co-education, therefore, must be unwise.

In the face of these re-iterated objections boys and girls study together in almost all Western colleges and universities. Side by side they study and recite in law, medicine, theology, languages, mathematics, and physics. The girls maintain good morals, good manners, and good health, with equal rank in scholarship. Presidents and professors, overseers, trustees, regents, and boards of examiners, all unite in unqualified testimony in favor of co-education. President

White of Cornell University, after an extended visit to all colleges in the West where co-education had been tried, wrote as follows: —

"If it be said that the presence of women will tend to lower the standard of scholarship, or at all events to keep the faculty from steadily raising it, it may be answered at once, that all the facts observed are in opposition to this view. The letters received by the committee, and their own recent observations in class-rooms, show, beyond a doubt, that the young women are at least equals of the young men in collegiate studies. As already stated, the best Greek scholar among the thirteen hundred students of the University of Michigan, a few years since, the best mathematical scholar in one of the largest classes of that institution to-day, and several among the highest in natural science, and in the general courses of study, are young women.

"The most concise and vigorous rendering from the most concise and vigorous of all — Tacitus himself — was given by a young lady at Oberlin College. Nor did the committee notice any better work in the most difficult of the great modern languages than that of some young women at Antioch College. Nor is our own university entirely without experience on this point. Among candidates for admission two years since no better examination was passed than that by a young lady, who had previously been successful in a competition for the State scholarship in one of the best educated counties of the State."

Rev. Dr. Fairchild, president of Oberlin College, says, "As to ability to maintain an excellent standing in college classes, that, during his own experience as professor, — eight years in ancient languages, Latin, Greek, and Hebrew; eleven in mathematics, abstract and applied; and eight in philosophical and ethical studies, — he has never observed any difference in the sexes as to performance in recitations. . . .

"Nor is there any manifest inability on the part of young women to endure the required labor. A breaking down in health does not appear to be more frequent than with young men. We have not observed a more frequent interruption of study on this account, nor do our statistics show a greater draught upon the vital forces in the case of those who have completed the full college course."

In answer to the question, whether young people will, under such a system, form such acquaintances as will result, during their course of study, or after they leave college, in matrimonial engagements, the doctor says, "Undoubtedly they will; and, if this is a fatal objection, the system must be pronounced a failure. The majority of young people form such acquaintances between the ages of sixteen and twenty-four, and these are the years devoted to a course of study. It would be a most unnatural state of things if such acquaintances should not be made. . . . The reasonable inquiry in the case is, whether such acquaintances and engagements can be made under circumstances more favorable to a wise and considerate adjustment, or more promising of a happy result."

A vast amount of similar testimony might be quoted from other eminent educators of the West, where co-education is very general, as well as from many of the successful instructors in the East. President Pierce of Rutgers College states the whole question in the following common-sense manner: "Surely there is nothing which the under-graduate learns in his college course, which he should not be glad that his wife should know as well as himself. Surely a liberal education has miserably failed of its aim when a man desires in a wife, not an equal, but a toy or slave. The idea of a woman as a slave is a barbarian idea. The savage has it to perfection, and because he has it he is a savage. The savage makes woman do the work of a beast of burden. The half-civilized Chinese puts on her all the drudgery of hard work: 'the wife drags the plough, the husband sows the grain.' To the savage, woman is a slave. The half-civilized man combines with this the idea of woman as a toy. This is an unchristian idea. Unhappily, it is too common, even with us; yet, with some other degrading ideas, it is a relic of heathenism. The whole difference between civilized Europe, half-civilized Asia, and savage Africa can be accurately measured by the idea of woman, — the best test of civilization in either a nation or an individual. The question, then, whether our civilization is to advance or retrograde — stand still it cannot — depends on the place hereafter to be given to woman. As to this question the present seems to be a sort of crisis. The signs point both ways. On the whole, the prospect is hopeful and cheering; but we must either go back, or go on; we must become either more Asiatic or more Christian."

There is one branch of higher education in which American women have little instruction. They are taught little concerning their own country, — its marvellous history, wherein its government differs from those of European nations, or what are the political issues pending at the time. Indeed this ignorance is considered creditable; and women in our country sometimes boast of it. It is otherwise in England. The intelligent women of the middle class in England — the class with which Americans are chiefly brought in contact — take a very lively interest in politics, know what are the public questions of the day, and are accurately informed concerning them. In the drawing-room, if politics form the topic of conversation among the gentlemen, you may expect the ladies to join in it intelligently and with spirit. They are ready with a defence of Gladstone's course in dealing with Ireland, or, if they think it defective or oppressive, they will tell you where and why. Since Church and State are one in England you will find them versed in the affairs of the English Church, even when they are nonconformists. They are familiar with colonial affairs, and have an opinion of their own concerning the wisdom or unwisdom, justice or injustice, of English management in India. And all the while they are never unwomanly, and you are held entranced by the charm of their intelligent speech.

It is surprising that the great body of American women rest contented in utter ignorance of the affairs of their country. For, if women are never to vote in America, — and this is by no means certain, since they are already voting in some States on school matters, — they will always be the mothers of voters. For mothers to renounce abjectly all hold upon their sons when they arrive at the voting age, and refuse to acquire the easily obtained information that would retain them the respect of the young men, and give them the ability still to counsel and advise, is very unnecessary self-abnegation. For them to be willingly, yes, gladly, indifferent and ignorant, when their own affairs are the subject of legislation, and laws are passed concerning their property and their children without their advice in the matter being asked, or their approval being sought, is to justify the category in which women are frequently mentioned, — "women, children, and *idiots.*" Not to know what were the horrors of a "Fugitive-slave Law," and the re-action which followed; what national purification is promised by a "civil-service reform;" what emancipation from the thraldom of strong drink by a "constitutional prohibitory amendment," — is to be unaware how great waves of uplifting float a state or a nation to a higher level, and how the world makes progress.

One woman of America, keeping watch of the political movements of her country, made the whole nation her debtor. For Harriet Beecher Stowe did for the hideous Fugitive-slave Law what Harriet Martineau did for the twenty-four laws of political economy, formulated in Adam Smith's "Wealth of Nations." She transformed it from a mass of tedious verbiage into a thrilling drama, the recital of which made the heart of the world palpitate with a desire for justice, and with divine pity for the slave. "An army with banners would have been a feeble re-enforcement to the abolition ranks," said Garrison, "compared with 'Uncle Tom's Cabin.'"

Other women there are to-day — not a large number as they "stand and are counted," but a host when estimated by the largeness of their moral purpose — who watch and weigh legislation in the interest of the advancement of their sex, and oppose it as it erects barriers to their progress. Others yet, whose idols of seeming fine gold have deteriorated to filthy clay under the debasing influence of the dram-shop, and who see the feet of their unwary sons caught early in the nets it spreads to catch them, have dried their useless tears, and are looking about for a remedy. When they discover that the dram-shop is protected by law, they organize their forces, and seek to change it. Is there any unwomanliness in such action?

There is no country like America. The youngest of the family of nations, its territorial area exceeds that of Rome when its empire was mightiest. "Europe, with her sixty empires, kingdoms, and republics, is only a sixth larger in extent." Its population of fifty millions includes all tongues, creeds, and races. Every nation on the globe sends us yearly a consignment of another million, who bring with them brawn and muscle, health, hope, and energy. The railroad and steamship, telegraph and telephone, make all these millions akin. Bankrupt in the start our country has in a century outstripped all nations in the acquisition of wealth, save one. Its resources are of every variety, and multiply infinitely. With all its imperfections its government is the freest, the noblest, the most humane, and the most just the world has ever seen. If the Roman declared his nationality with pride, the American may announce his with pride and thanksgiving; for America is

> "The mother with the ever open door,
> The feet of many nations on her floor,
> And room for all the world about her knees."

In this great and growing Anglo-American empire, whose far-reaching future no prophet's eye can see, women stand on higher vantage-ground than ever before. Never since the world began have they been so honored, so loved, so privileged, so free, and so trusted. Let us admit this, while deploring the injustice still meted out to them, and the curtailment of freedom and opportunity, of which their brothers have the fullest measure. For this wrong hastens to its overthrow. American men, who are in the main noble in their relations with women, believe in "fair play." And a great under-current is bearing women into larger life and higher fields of effort. What they do, and what they are, is to tell as never before on the national character.

A young Brahmin, visiting England, expressed his astonishment at her advanced civilization. "Why is it," he inquired of his companion, an enlightened Englishman, "that India has stood still these last eight or ten centuries, while England has made such astounding progress in the arts and sciences, and in good government?"

## Higher Education.

His companion gave him a *résumé* of the underlying causes of modern civilization, and concluded as follows: "In addition your women are children even to old age, and do not stimulate men, but hold them back. But the women of the Occident are learning to keep step with men in scientific pursuits, a knowledge of art, and a study of social problems; and this is a stimulant to men to go farther." If the partial education of women has been productive of such good results, how much might be hoped for if women shared with men every opportunity for growth, and every incentive to noble achievement!

Then let our young girls be encouraged to acquaint themselves with the great questions that engage the attention of our government, — and especially with those that are discussed in congresses, legislatures, and by the leading papers of the time. Let them know what are the social and educational movements of the day, and what is their bearing on the future of the nation. Great moral principles underlie them all. Talk with them about the sectional wrongs that should be righted, the great reforms that are battling with injustice, the needed legislation that is pending and slowly progressing. These matters can be made as interesting to them as Greek literature or Roman history, as fascinating as the everlasting novel. Brief political monographs, terse, clear, and compact, are prepared by specialists and college professors for the instruction of our young legal voters. Let them enter into the studies of their sisters, who will find some knowledge of the great problems with which a nation wrestles as powerful a tonic mentally, as are physically, the out-door games they share with their brothers.

Rev. Dr. Mark Hopkins, the beloved and venerable president of Williams College, Massachusetts, in 1875 wrote as follows: "I would at this point correct my teaching in 'The Law of Love,' to the effect that home is peculiarly the sphere of woman, and civil government that of man. I now regard the home as the joint sphere of man *and* woman, and *the sphere of civil government more of an open question between the two.*" A concession of this kind from so eminent an authority as Rev. Dr. Hopkins indicates a great change in public opinion. It shows which way the changing current is setting. Not more than twenty years ago I heard an educated and cultivated woman advise her audience of nearly fifteen hundred women to "hold themselves so aloof from politics, that they would be unaware of the name of the governor of their State, or of the President of the United States." Her stultifying advice was received with "immense applause;" and the daily press of the city, in its next day's report, sagely commended "the wisdom of the eminent speaker."

No public speaker would dare proffer such advice to women now; for they have felt the pressure of civil government very heavily these last twenty years. They have given fathers and brothers, husbands and sons, to die in a political war, waged for the destruction of the national life. Driven to self-support their burdens have been increased by taxation, levied to pay the war-debt of the country. The flood-gates of demoralization, which the war opened wide, have let in on them sorrow and disaster, surpassing that wrought by the long conflict between the North and the South, through the legal protection extended to the manufacture and sale of intoxicating drinks, which the war immensely stimulated. And the conviction is rapidly gaining ground, that women ought be more than the victims of government. "I go for all sharing the privileges of the government," said Abraham Lincoln, "who assist in bearing its burdens, — by no means excluding women." And while a host of men and women content themselves with the utterance of this belief, another host move steadily forward towards the practical realization of this doctrine. Not to know of these movements in the mother-land, whose children we are, is to fall into the rear of the onward-marching column. It is to defraud ourselves of a great mental stimulus, and to rob ourselves of the invigorating hope that the future holds for our daughters a fuller, nobler, and completer life than the past could give to their mothers.

## CHAPTER IV.

NEED OF PRACTICAL TRAINING.

Our social structure has been based on the theory that "all men support all women," — a theory which has never been true, and which is farther from being true to-day than ever before. Consequently, boys have been educated to have some well-defined, clear-cut purpose in life. The widest range of education has been open to them; and the whole world of culture, work, and business has invited them. It has been, and is still, regarded as a misfortune, when a boy grows to manhood, aimless, shiftless, content to live on the labor of others. With girls it has been otherwise. It has been assumed that they would marry, and be "supported" by tender and competent husbands. The only training necessary to them, therefore, it has been assumed, should be such as would fit them to be wives, mothers, and housekeepers, — "sweet dependants," held perpetually in "soft subjection."

The practical working of this theory has weighted women with heavy disabilities; for many men make neither good nor competent husbands. Many are incompetent, others are invalids, some are dissolute and idle, and not a few desert entirely both wives and children. Many women who have husbands find themselves compelled to aid in earning the means of living; many wives earn the entire livelihood of the whole family. Many women are widows, while an increasingly large number in the Eastern and Middle States do not marry at all. Untaught in any industry, utterly lacking in practical knowledge, ignorant of the simplest forms of business, they suffer great hardships. Many women left widows, with property to care for, because of their ignorance of business, become the victims of gross injustice. They fall an easy prey to the dishonest and designing, who, under pretence of assisting them, pluck them like geese.

It is of this last class that Miss Cobbe speaks, who says, "At sixty, when their husbands die, they are no better able to manage their affairs than they were at six, but betray by their childishness that the whole moral work of life has been stopped for them for half a century. My father used to laugh at such widows, and said they reminded him of clocks with the weights taken off, which instantly set off, buzz! buzz! buzz! till they ran down."

As the theory that "all men support all women" does not fit the facts it is time for us to reform our theory as well as our practice. I would give to all girls equal intellectual and industrial training with boys. I would not give them the same training unless they were fitting for the same work, business, or profession; but I would, in all cases, give to them equal advantages. If I were able, I would change the public sentiment so radically, that no girl should be considered well-educated, no matter what her accomplishments, until she had learned a trade, a business, a vocation, or a profession. Self-support would then be possible to her, and she would not float on the current of life, a part of its useless driftwood, borne hither and thither by its troubled waters. There would then be fewer heavily taxed fathers and brothers, toiling like galley-slaves to support healthy and vigorous human beings in stagnating idleness,—idle for no earthly reason than that God has made them women. Society has a claim upon every human being, women as well as men, for some useful work, in return for the support and protection it affords them. Girls would then escape one of the most serious dangers to which inefficient women are liable, — the danger of regarding marriage as a means of livelihood.

"But there are many men with large incomes, abundantly able to support their daughters, without being at all taxed: would you have these daughters of rich men trained to self-support?" I am asked.

In our country, who is rich? The financial world — and in one sense the political — is a huge fandango. Now you are up, and then you are down. You are rich to-day; you are poor to-morrow. It is not possible to entail estates as in England; and there are very few American families in possession of wealth inherited through two or three generations. If women do not know it, men are keenly alive to the fact that it is much easier in America to make money than to invest it where it will be secure from loss, and will steadily yield a moderate sum for income. Every financial convulsion topples over some of the kings of trade and commerce, who, in their fall, pull others down by the hundreds. Every man's financial ruin involves women in disaster, who, unless they are exceptionally brave or technically trained, hang about his neck like mill-stones, dragging him hopelessly under.

We hear continually of women who were born into wealth, and who were reared in elegant dependence. But the men who furnished the means on which they lived in inactive luxury have been wrecked in some speculation, or in some business panic; and they have suffered wreck also. Then comes the effort to provide for them,—an effort in many cases utterly futile. A home in Washington City provides for many of these impoverished elderly gentlewomen, and was established for this purpose. To hear the histories of some of these women from their own lips is to listen to a tragic illustration of the maxim, that "to be weak is to be miserable." Reared to cling to others for support, like the ivy to the oak when the oak has fallen, they have gone down with it, helpless to rise again. The same lesson can be learned from many of the women filling offices in government departments, who turn pale and faint when a messenger enters the room where they are at work, bearing in his hand a package of yellow envelopes. Within some of these envelopes may be folded their dismissal from their positions.

And if the beneficiaries of the Boston fund, — who receive a weekly stipend of two dollars, when their parents have been taxpayers in the city, and they have dropped into such indigence as to need charity, — if most of these should tell their stories even here in New England, it would be only a reiteration of the same oft-told tale. "My father was one of the richest men in Boston," said one of these poor, gentle-ladies: "we were taught only accomplishments, and often heard our mother say there would always be money in plenty to support us handsomely. How to get a living was a subject that neither my sisters nor myself ever heard discussed; and when our mother's death followed swiftly on our father's failure it was too late for us to learn any trade or business. We have dragged along miserably, doing a little when we could, and helped by our friends as they have been able; all the while drifting steadily into hopeless poverty and helpless old age."

Naturalists tell us that "a lobster, left high and dry among the rocks, has not instinct and energy enough to work his way back to the sea,

## Need of Practical Training. 65

but waits for the sea to come to him. If it does not come, he remains where he is, and dies; although the slightest effort would enable him to reach the waves, which are, perhaps, tossing and tumbling within a yard of him." Is it not pitiful that we rear young girls as if they were "human lobsters," which, when stranded on the rocks or the shore, must wait for some friendly wave to float them again?

But lack of technical and industrial training not only makes dependent and inefficient women of our daughters, it puts them in fearful peril morally. Indolence is always demoralizing. It ruins health, destroys beauty, and enfeebles the will. When temptation comes, in the prospect of a life of ease, although coupled with dishonor, it is potent to allure an indolent, light-hearted, frivolous young woman, unless nature has endowed her with superior moral instinct. She yields to the lure; and, instead of the freedom and happiness promised, she enters into abject slavery and remediless woe. From the earthly hell into which she has fallen, society allows no escape. It calls her a "lost woman," and with unchristian treatment aims to make its atheistic statement true.

"Out of two thousand fallen women in the city

of New York eighteen hundred and eighty had
been brought up '*to do nothing;*' five hundred
and twenty-five pleaded destitution as the cause
of their sad life; and all but fifty-one had been
religiously educated."

"The public are responsible for this evil," says
Dr. Sanger, who has written exhaustively on this
subject, "because they persist in excluding women
from many kinds of employment for which they
are fitted; while, for work that is open, they receive inadequate compensation. The community
are equally responsible for non-interference with
acknowledged evils."

Not very long since a paper was read at the
annual meeting of the "Association for the Advancement of Women," entitled "A Plea for
Fallen Women." Its author, a philanthropic
woman, had had large experience with the class
of whom she wrote, working with rare wisdom
and unselfishness. I quote one paragraph of her
paper: —

"If we could realize that inherent weakness
of character among women, more than inherent
grossness, leads them to adopt this sad career
with its tragical close, we should feel that as
women we have great responsibilities in the mat-

## Need of Practical Training. 67

ter. Vast multitudes of women lead abandoned lives to-day. The population of public women in New York is that of one to every five hundred and eighteen; in Paris, one to every two hundred and eighty-one; in Chicago, one to every two hundred and thirty." (The residence of this lady is Chicago.)

"Statistics seem to show that the evil diminishes as means of employment are opened to women, and opportunities given them to support themselves honorably. In Birmingham and Sheffield, Eng., — the two cities of the world where most employments are open to women, — only one in seven hundred and nine leads an abandoned life, — the lowest proportion found anywhere except at the Hague. Every endeavor, then, which women make to open new fields of industry for women, and to fit them to labor therein, is a direct blow at this hydra-headed monster, which preys so devouringly on our social life. Every industrial school which we open for girls, every industrial bureau we establish for women, protects them against this terrible future contingency."

In view of these facts, which might be multiplied indefinitely, and with which all persons who have-had any experience of life are familiar, ought not all mothers, and all intrusted with the training of young girls, to demand for them a more symmetrical education? Ought we not to rid ourselves of the inherited social idea, that it is a shameful thing for young women to be taught to support themselves by honorable industry? Is it not time to cease the protest against their being fitted to lead individual, earnest, responsible lives?

In an early stage of the last war, before the government had learned its resources, or organized its various departments, I saw a body of soldiers march from Benton Barracks, the St. Louis camp of rendezvous, and embark on boats to go down the Mississippi. Among them were companies — and I am not certain but regiments — without uniforms and without equipments. The men wore the citizen's dress in which they had enlisted. It was explained that they had been ordered to the front immediately after enlistment in advance of the arrival of their uniforms and guns. Their presence was necessary to maintain the *morale* of the army, which was unfavorably affected by the mustering-out of large numbers who had enlisted on short terms

## Need of Practical Training. 69

of service, — " three-months' men," " nine-months' men," and " fifteen-months' men." This had greatly depleted the ranks at certain points, and infected those left behind, not yet used to war, with a very demoralizing homesickness. Uniforms, guns, and the all-important drill would be given these raw recruits, we were told, when they reached their destination.

Two or three weeks later I met some of these very unequipped men, still without uniforms, on board a hospital boat, steaming slowly up the river, then at its highest stage of water. It was *en route* for the superb general hospitals of St. Louis with a sad freight of wounded soldiers. Some of the poor fellows were so broken in body, so rent with shot and shell, that their own mothers would not have recognized them. I heard their pitiful story from many lips in many versions, but it was always the same story. Hardly had these green boys in the clothing of civilians reached their regiments, when they were surprised by the enemy; and without guns, or an hour's drill, they were plunged into a sharp, disastrous engagement. Shot at, shot down, they could make no defence; for they had not been supplied with the munitions of war, nor taught how to use them. The officers in command dashed up and down the lines, exhorting the men to steadiness and bravery with a very agony of earnestness; but the language of war was foreign to these poor fellows. They did not understand what was meant.

Others, equally unfortunate, whose equipments had arrived in season, were at a fearful disadvantage from ignorance of their use and of military tactics. Seeking to follow their comrades, who were older soldiers, and had before been under fire, they became entangled among themselves, and were brought under the galling, raking fire of their own batteries, which mowed them down in long, bleeding swaths, as grass falls before the scythe in June.

It is as wasteful, as unwise, as inhuman, to send our delicately nurtured and tenderly reared young daughters out from the home to fight the battle of life without a preparation for it, without an equipment in the form of an industrial and business education, as it was to send these hapless young fellows to fight the enemy without drill and without guns. The results are more disastrous, and reach farther. Our daughters are not shot down, like the untrained military recruit: they live, but with no individual grasp on life.

They become anxious concerning the future, with no power to provide for it. At the mercy of circumstances which they know not how to control; victims of petty beliefs, old abuses, and respectable tyrannies; afraid to step out of ancient ruts, and scared at the innovation of new truths, — they drop into mental un-health, and bodily disease comes with it. All the while the world goes forward, and they stand still. And frequently, long before death comes, they are consigned to the grave of oblivion, without even the courtesy of funeral ceremonies.

Or they marry, and make faithful, loving, lovely wives to admiring husbands. But the husband dies. He was living on a salary, which ceases with his life. Or he had just commenced business, and the settlement of his affairs leaves nothing for his family. His young widow has one or more children. What is she to do if she be without relatives or friends to fall back upon, who may perhaps be carrying all the burdens they know how to bear? Or the husband may drop into permanent invalidism, or into bankruptcy, or into dissolute habits. If the young wife has not been in part prepared for such emergencies by previous training, her lot is hard indeed.

"Oh, you can't prepare girls to meet such emergencies!" said an eminent clergyman, in whose parlors this topic was being earnestly discussed. "You must prepare them to be good, practical wives and mothers, and risk the rest. There you will have to leave them, and trust in God."

Our trust must be in God, to be sure. No one disputes that. And yet I have the deepest respect for the advice that Oliver Cromwell gave his soldiers, — " Trust in God, *and keep your powder dry !* "

Prepare our daughters to be good wives, mothers, and home-makers! Do we systematically attempt this? Do we conduct the education of girls with this object? Do we not trust almost entirely to natural instinct and aptitude, which, in the woman, is incomparably strong in the direction of wifehood, motherhood, and the home? For the mighty reason that the majority of women will always while the world stands be wives, mothers, and mistresses of homes, they should receive the largest, completest, and most thorough training. It is not possible to state this too strongly. For these positions are the most important that woman can occupy. Education, religion, human affection, and civil law, all

## Need of Practical Training. 73

should conspire to aid her in these departments to do the best work of which she is capable.

The very highest function of woman is to raise and train the family: it is the very highest function of man also. Indeed civilization has but this end in view, — the perpetuation and improvement of the race. The establishment of homes, the rearing of families, the founding of schools and colleges, the planting of institutions, the maintaining of governments, all are but means to this end. As Humboldt said years ago, "Governments, religion, property, books, are but the scaffolding to build men. Earth holds up to her Master no fruit, but the finished man."

The most important agency of all these is the home. For here the very foundation is laid for future good or evil. The first step away from animalism is taken when a human being, young or old, is established in a well-ordered home. The advance of a nation comes only through the improvement of the homes of the nation. As the aggregate of these may be, so will the nation be. For it is here that the real humanizing and civilizing is carried forward. As a rule the worth or the worthlessness of the home is the work of woman. "A man may build a castle or a palace," says Miss Cobbe, "but, poor creature! be he wise as Solomon and rich as Crœsus, he cannot turn it into a home. No masculine mortal can do that. It is a woman, and only a woman, — a woman, all by herself, if she likes, and without any man to help her, — who can turn a house into a home."

Are the duties of motherhood so slight and easy of right performance that no preparation or training is necessary? Are the qualities and aptitudes that go towards the making of a good home normal to all young women? And are they as certain of success as is the bird when she begins to build her nest? We are all familiar with the witty saying of Oliver Wendell Holmes: "There are people who think that every thing may be done, if the doer, be he educator or physician, be only called 'in season.' No doubt: but *in season* would often be a hundred or two years before the child was born, and people never send so early as that."

The duties of the mother begin long before her child comes into life, — ay, and the duties of the father also. She needs to know all that science can teach of the pre-natal laws of being, and of the laws of heredity. Her acquaintance with physiology should not be the superficial knowledge given in the ordinary school or college even. It should be a thorough exposition of the mysteries of her own physical being, with a clear statement of the hygienic laws she must obey, if she would grow into healthy, enduring, glorious womanhood. She should be taught the laws of ventilation and nutrition; what constitutes healthful food; the care of infancy; the nursing of the sick; and in what that vigilant and scrupulous cleanliness consists, which almost prohibits certain forms of disease from passing under one's roof.

The details of this necessary knowledge can only be learned in practice, and slowly; but the foundations must be laid in early study. The mother must dignify these matters in the mind of her daughter, by her own observance of them; and there are pouring in upon us such floods of light pertaining to all matters of physical life and well-being, that the mothers of the future, in these respects, ought to be a great improvement on the mothers of the past and present.

What are the qualities that go towards the making of a home that are necessary to good housekeeping? Intelligence, system, economy, industry, patience, good-nature, firmness, good health, a fine moral sense, all these are called into action. So is a knowledge of cooking, laundry-work, how to make and repair clothing, together with the other industries of domestic life, even when one has means to employ servants to perform this work; for a woman cannot tell when she is well served, unless she knows what good work is. It requires a very high order of woman to be a good wife, mother, and housekeeper; and she who makes a success in these departments possesses such a combination of admirable qualities, both mental and moral, that, with proper training, she might make a success in almost any department.

No wonder that Theodore Parker, in his discourse on "The Public Function of Woman," nearly thirty years ago, argued that she should be admitted to participate in public affairs because of her great success in the domestic world. He said, "Government is political economy, — *national housekeeping.* Does any respectable woman keep house as badly as the United States? with so much bribery, so much corruption, so much quarrelling, in the domestic councils? . . . After women have done all that pertains to housekeeping as a trade, and as one of the fine arts; after they have done all for the order of the house, of the husband and children, — they have still energies to spare, a reserved power for other work. . . . In government as housekeeping, or government as morality, I think man makes a very poor appearance when he says woman could not do as well as he has done, and is doing."

We have much to say of the power which the man has over his wife; but is it greater, albeit it is different, than that which the wife has over the husband? President Dwight, of Yale College, was wont to say that a man must ask his wife if he may be rich. And all know the truth behind that sententious statement. "If Heaven allotted to each man seven guardian angels," said Lord Lytton, "five of them ought to be hovering night and day over his pockets; for the management of money is, in much, the managing of one's self." Not unfrequently the five angels of the pocket seem to reside in the wife, whose wise economy fills the house with comfort, sends sons and daughters to college, clears the homestead from mortgage, and all from the very moderate income of the husband. I need not look far from my study window for a practical illustration of this. But when there is a lack of this homely virtue in the wife, and when from ignorance or recklessness she rushes into extravagance, which the income does not warrant, there is hindrance for the children, embarrassment for the husband, and poverty for the household.

We condemn severely, and justly, the man who, from his vices or his ill-temper and tyranny, is a terror to his family, a loathing to his wife. But is the sottish, sensual, vile-tempered husband so unbearable a calamity as is a wife of the same dreadful pattern? Thank God! there are comparatively few such wives in America. One shudders, and grows sick at heart, to remember how numerous are the debauched women one sees among the low classes of Great Britain. The memory of drunken mothers, reeling out of London gin-palaces at midnight, with little children clinging to their skirts; of infuriate mothers, frenzied with whiskey, fighting in the back streets of Dublin, and in their insensate rage treading down the little toddlers that clutched at their rags and called them by endearing names: one struggles against it as against a nightmare. The wretchedness of that household, at whose head is an immoral, depraved wife and mother, is indescribable.

Because of the vast importance of the domestic

function of woman, and of its far-reaching influence; because she stands so near the beginnings of life that she, more than the father, plants the impulses which last the longest and are most deeply rooted, — all women should have an early training commensurate with the greatness of the work that only they can perform. Let our young daughters be garnished with accomplishments, if you will. Let them have amusements, and live and breathe in a sunny, gay atmosphere. Encourage them to cultivate that habit of looking at the best and brightest side of things, which Dr. Johnson has pronounced "worth a thousand pounds a year." Do not repress their girlish enthusiasm over their pursuits or their pleasures. They will have need of a large store before they are done with life. Give to them the highest education demanded by the hunger of their souls, and allow them to fit for any calling or profession to which they are adapted by their tastes and capacities.

But by no means neglect what Canon Kingsley calls their "lower education." Let them have an acquaintance with themselves, with their own physiology, and the laws controlling it. Let them be trained, as far as possible, as if you were sure they were to be wives, mothers, and housekeepers, even when they receive, in addition, technical training. But few women reach adult life, even when they do not marry, without finding themselves so circumstanced at times that a domestic training is invaluable to them. Thus will our daughters be prepared to do better work in the home, to rear nobler children. Trained and self-poised, they will not be in bondage to ignorance; nor will they be as liable to become the dupes or the prey of others. A wife and mother should always be mistress of herself and of her department, and never the slave of another, — not even when that other is her husband, and the slavery is founded on her undying love. That robs her of half her value. "Give your child to be educated by a slave," said the old Greek, "and, instead of one slave, you will then have two."

I have an ideal of the motherhood of the future. Its realization must wait till invention has simplified household as it has agricultural labor, or till co-operation extends to housekeeping as it has to business. It must tarry till the common-sense of the community shall demand that women be trained to good physical health, and to the intellectual development that shall fit them for their work. We need not look for it while woman is held in bondage to her own passions, or those of another, nor where enlightened motherhood lacks the complement of enlightened fatherhood. We must wait for it till marriages are based on love, respect, and equality; and the twain are drawn together by harmonial tastes and temperaments. With it will come to man "the statelier Eden." Then will human motherhood—and human fatherhood—take on something of the fulness, tenderness, and divineness of Godhood. And then will the children, born into their home, have trooping about them such divinities as were never throned on old Olympus.

## CHAPTER V.

### INDUSTRIAL AND TECHNICAL TRAINING.

No phase of the great movement for the advancement of women progresses so slowly as that which demands their technical and industrial training. To be sure, the last thirty years, which have brought great changes to the women of America, have largely increased the number of remunerative employments they are permitted to enter. When Harriet Martineau visited America in 1840 she found but seven employments open to women. They could teach, do any kind of needlework (including tailoring, dressmaking, and millinery), keep boarders, work in cotton-mills, set type, fold and stitch in book-binderies, and go out to household service. The women of Massachusetts are now working in two hundred and eighty-four occupations; and 251,158 are earning their living in them, receiving from one hundred and fifty dollars to three thousand dollars each every year. This computation does not include amateurs, nor mothers and daughters in the household, and, of course, excludes domestic service. It is true, however, that women have received very little special industrial training to fit them for the work they are doing, or for a higher kind of work which will give them better pay. Perhaps almost the same may be said concerning the technical training of men in this country.

For education in America for both boys and girls has been mainly literary. While our public schools have been the pride of the century, and are justly regarded as the corner-stone of our liberties, — since a republican government cannot live with an illiterate or an immoral constituency behind it, — there is to-day a growing dissatisfaction with our system of popular education. It is for the head, and not for the hands. It does not bear directly on the pursuits of the people. We have shaped our school and academy courses as if the college were the certain goal of all the pupils. Consequently children who are to live by manual labor are engaged in studies which have little or no bearing on their future occupation. They drop out from the public school, at various points, under the pressure of need, or because they must acquire the industrial skill necessary to obtain a livelihood, taking with them only fragments of an education designed to fit other children for a higher school or the college. There should be maintained at the public cost schools for the training of children in useful trades, as well as schools for their preparation for college. An earnest demand is being made that popular education shall be brought into harmony with the times, and the requirements of labor; that industrial training shall in some way be engrafted on our school-system. This demand is not a temporary one, and will not rest until something is done to meet it; for the interests of the community demand that children who are to earn their livelihood by their hands shall have an education to fit them for their work.

It has become an absolute necessity of our present social condition that young women should have free admission to professional and industrial training; indeed that no girl should be regarded as well educated, no matter what her acquirements, till she is in possession of a trade, a profession, a craft, or an accomplishment, by which she can maintain herself if it be necessary. Notwithstanding the increased number of occupations opened to women during the last quarter

## Industrial and Technical Training. 85

of a century there are yet too few for those who have need of them. All are crowded with applicants, except the professions of medicine, the law, and the ministry, or those employments demanding skilled labor. These applicants, competing with one another for place, tread each other down, and keep wages at a minimum.

It is not wholly the fault of the capitalist that women are so poorly paid for their labor. Any article sells cheap when there is too much of it in the market; and woman's labor is cheap, because, in part, it is largely unskilled, and because too much of it is forced on the market. Take the profession of teaching. Everywhere the salaries of women are much below those of men. Why? Not because they are less successful than men in the same profession, or do less work or poorer work. Nor yet, as some affirm, because they have entered the profession temporarily, as a stepping-stone to something better; for this is no more the truth concerning women than men teachers. And, if some leave it to marry, it must be remembered that many school boards dismiss women teachers who venture on matrimony. The truth is, there are too many women teachers. Fewer young women should qualify for the over-crowded profession of teaching, but should fit for other skilled employments. But what others are there? Instead of forcing women to compete with men in the same employments, when, as a rule, they are compelled to do the same work for less pay, a wiser way is to open to women new industries, and to provide for them new employments. A movement in this direction is already well begun in our country.

I can recall the large expectations with which my heart dilated, as I journeyed to the Centennial Exposition of 1876 held in Philadelphia. For to me the chief attraction of the great "International Exhibition" was the "Woman's Department," and to that my thoughts persistently travelled. Once inside the turn-stile, and fairly on the grounds, I disregarded the directions of my companion, who had preceded me to the Exhibition, and had learned what was the order of sight-seeing to be observed that would best economize time and strength. "Do not annoy me with importunity," was my entreaty; "for I cannot enjoy the Main Building nor Horticultural Hall till I have paid my respects to the Woman's Department." And to the Woman's Department we went. Of course

I was doomed to disappointment. Like many another disappointed visitor my imagination had outrun the possibilities of the occasion.

The "Woman's Building" was barren of all exterior decoration, — solid, substantial, severely practical in its architecture. The other Exposition buildings clustering about it were of an airy lightness, glowing in color, and graceful in form. One felt wronged that the architect of the building for women had made it so severely simple, so rigidly utilitarian; and many were prejudiced against the department before they had entered it. "Why did not the architect embody in this 'Woman's Pavilion' his fairest dream of beauty?" was a universal query. Inside there was an incompleteness and a paucity painfully oppressive. Much of the handicraft of women was in the other buildings, where it could not be classified, as it was complementing the skill of men. Many of the women exhibitors preferred a classification of work rather than of sex, and were exhibiting in the Main Building or in Machinery Hall or in the Art Gallery. Many were prevented from making any exhibit whatever, from lack of means to work out their ideas in an attractive form; and so it came about that the Woman's Department was very unsatisfactory, and utterly failed to show to the world what woman was doing in the line of work.

There was no lack of needlework, embroidery, and worsted work; but much of it was a weariness to the eye. The birds and butterflies, the flowers and ferns, were so utterly unlike any thing seen in nature. There was "spatter-work" and "tatting," wax-work and hair-work, bead-work and feather-work, lace-work and muslin-work, and every other conceivable form of fancy-work. There were inventions that had secured patents; but very naturally they related entirely to household work. There was a "lap-table" and a "complete darner," "a self-locking barrel-cover" and a "complete rolling-pin," a "washing-machine" and a "dress-protector," an "invalid's bed" and a "sewing-machine treadle," and so on. None of them were of any great value. There was machinery run by women, which wove carpets, shawls, scarfs, hoods, cloaks, and fabrics of worsted, and mixed silk and wool; but one can see work of this kind performed in many manufacturing towns. There was an art gallery, where the pictures exhibited by women were about as "good, bad, and indifferent" as were those exhibited by men of all nations

## Industrial and Technical Training. 89

in Memorial Hall. Everywhere there was a vast deal of "pretty pettiness," which set forth, in unmistakable language, how small and few have been the methods by which women in the past have obtained a living.

But yet, with all its many disappointments, there was much in this Woman's Department to awake thankfulness. The women students of the Philadelphia Woman's Medical College proved their ability to set up as apothecaries by their remarkably fine *materia medica* exhibits. The beautifully carved furniture from Cincinnati was a great surprise, revealing the possibilities of woman in a new and remunerative field of artistic industry. The various schools of design gave promise of new openings to women when they have received education in industrial art; and I lingered entranced over the wood-carving, decorated china, painted tiles, crayons, and the marvellous designs for carpets, wall-papers, oil-cloths, calicoes, lace, and other articles of manufacture, — all the work of the students in these schools. A weekly paper was published in the building; the editorial work most ably done by cultivated women, the type-setting and printing equally well done by skilled women, — both together combining to furnish an almost perfect eight-paged weekly paper that all read with delight.

A farmer's wife from Arkansas exhibited an ideal head, modelled in butter, at which people laughed because of the unconventional material, and around which they hung in admiration because of the rare artistic skill. Canova, as a boy, modelled in butter; but, as a man, discarded it for clay. But this woman refused to work in other material. I heard of a woman engineer, who ran the steam-engine which worked the machinery and printing-press of the Woman's Department, and went to the little engine-room to see her. I found a comely young maiden with pleasant face, refined manner, and dainty dress, who, amid the heat, dust, smoke, and noise, preserved her neatness and lady-like bearing, and yet did all the work "from starting the fire in the morning to blowing off steam at night." She said that "her labor was not so exhausting as taking charge of an ordinary cook-stove, while her pay was twelve dollars per week." This woman engineer was one of the most notable exhibitions of the Woman's Department. Crowds continually gathered about her to ask questions. And almost every man engineer on the grounds took his turn in calling

## Industrial and Technical Training. 91

on her, generally professing that he was going to "quiz" her. If he undertook the quizzing, his experience was like that of another man, of whom we have read, "who went out shearing, but went home shorn." For her dignity and self-poise were a sure protection against discourtesy.

After a time I went to the Main Building; and, walking up and down amid its wonders and glories, I asked questions and received answers. Everywhere I was shown the work of women, — lace, pottery, porcelain, silverware, glassware, every variety of textile fabric, embroidered in exquisite designs, every variety of wood-carving and painting on wood, carpets, rugs, watches, screens worked in *appliqué* from Japan, or painted in fantastic designs, and glowing colors, from China, — until I finally said, "Here in this Main Building is the Woman's Department, and not in the Woman's Building." In every department of the Exposition the handicraft of woman was to be found; and much that men exhibited, as proprietors of establishments or manufactories, proved, on investigation, to have been wrought by women. I found I could make a magnificent Woman's Department, if I could eliminate, from the Main Building alone, the articles of women's manufacture. And so packed was this airy, crystal structure with works of value and beauty, the handiwork of man, that nothing would then appear to have been subtracted, and it would still have challenged the wonder and admiration of all visitors. But this was the sorrowful result of my investigations. In this new Woman's Department, which I could have constructed, I should have needed but small space for the work of my countrywomen. What was the explanation?

Not that American women are inferior to those of Europe. In some respects they are superior, and they are more happily conditioned. They are freer. Men respect and prize them more highly, and care for them more tenderly. They have a fine basis of intellectual culture, lacking in most of the foreign women artisans; they have greater adaptability to circumstances, and greater celerity of mental movement; they have an intense love of the beautiful, and exquisite taste, which, for lack of other methods of expression, show themselves now, mainly, in graceful dress and household decoration; and they are surrounded by beautiful forms in nature, which are vainly sought abroad. But in our country there are few schools of design for women, and fewer technical schools, such as abound in Europe, where art and science are taught as applied to industry. The Massachusetts Institute of Technology has recently opened its doors to young women; and the Illinois Industrial University affords women a more comprehensive industrial training than any other institution in our country.

But in the Old World the schools of design and the technical schools that admit women to study industrial art are very numerous, and of great value. For the nations of Europe contend with one another for industrial, as well as national, supremacy. There are *millions of men and women* in the manufacturing establishments of the Old World, and in its workshops, who have been trained for years in art and science as applied to industry. Why should not the work of these women surpass in beauty of design, and excellence of finish, that of American women? It would be marvellous, indeed, if it were otherwise. In addition these European art-schools are generally established by government, instruction is given in many of them free of charge, and they are abundantly supported by appropriations from the national exchequer.

The South-Kensington Museum was founded in

London some thirty years ago at an expense to the government of some six millions of dollars. It appropriates annually a million and a half more for its maintenance. The buildings of the museum already cover twelve acres, and in time will cover sixty or seventy more; for the government continues to gather into it whatever is rare and beautiful and valuable from all parts of the world. Its well-packed showcases now cover acres, and its picture-lined corridors are miles in extent, so that its future size and value must be immense. A hundred thousand students are admitted yearly, who receive instruction in fine and industrial art, and are admitted to the almost boundless resources of the museum with every facility for studying and copying. There are more women students than men; and, while each sex has its separate class and practising rooms, the lecture-room, library, examination-room, and museum are common to both. "The success of the women students," says Professor Walter Smith, late State director of art-education in Massachusetts, "to put it in the very mildest form, is greater than that of the male students. And this in face of infinitely greater difficulties, arising from limitation of subjects of study, and other distinctions, which need not be referred to by me."

From this great art-centre at South Kensington art-instruction radiates to every part of the kingdom of Great Britain. Its influence is felt in the increasingly artistic character of the local manufactures, in the promotion of machine and building construction, the improvement of architecture, and the elevation of the public taste. Its benefits are within the reach of all; the Government regarding the money thus expended as a necessary and wise investment, which pays handsomely in developing the genius of the English people.

Other nations are carrying forward the same industrial art-training on a scale less grand, — France, Germany, Austria, Italy, Denmark, Spain, even little Portugal, even barbaric Russia. For while soldiers are still drilled in European camps children and youth are being trained in European schools to artistic labor as never before. An age of industrial rivalry has set in; and, as Carlyle states it, "The true epic of our times is, not arms and the man, but *tools* and the man, — an infinitely wider kind of epic."

No such provision as this exists in the United States, and the deficiency is supplied by private or corporate action, when supplied at all. Many students, not only of high art, but of industrial art, are obliged to expatriate themselves, and study in Europe. The wealth hitherto attained by our country has been mainly due to her natural resources, and the ingenuity which has developed them. The United States have largely furnished raw materials for the rest of the world, and their manufactures have not called for a high degree of skill or taste.

But a nation that is content to deal chiefly in raw materials, and to do only coarse and rude kinds of work, must remain forever at a disadvantage with other nations, which educate labor, and give to it skill. It will be practically a "hewer of wood, and a drawer of water," for them. That nation is richest whose artisans can, by educated skill and taste, transform its natural products into the largest variety of articles which the world can use, and for which it can pay. The great secret of the prosperity of France lies in the fact that she buys materials cheaply wherever she can find them, and then, through the marvellous taste and skill of her educated artisans, transforms them into articles that have beauty of design and rare finish, so that they are

## Industrial and Technical Training. 97

sought in all the markets of the world. To advertise a fabric or a utensil as "French" is in advance to bespeak for it a ready sale; and this is due to the fact that the skill of the French artisan gives great value to the materials out of which it is made. France is in this way always able to sell more than she buys; consequently enriches herself, and lifts herself out of financial trouble easily, as she did after the disastrous Franco-Prussian war.

How different in America! Every manufacturer knows that his wares, to be salable, must not only be of good material, but must possess beauty of design, be the article a carpet or a wall-paper, a goblet or a water-jug. But in the majority of cases, to obtain this desirable quality, the American manufacturer must import the designer or the design. Because of our poverty of art-culture, as expressed in our architecture, furniture, and fabrics, we import millions of dollars' worth of goods from the Old World every year, — cameos, pictures, bronzes, and statuary; silks, laces, velvets, and carpets; china, porcelain, pottery, and glass-ware; designs for our manufactures, and drawings to work from.

"Every branch of our manufactures," says

Professor Ware, late of the Boston School of Technology, "is suffering from the want of intelligence and skill."

"Only by developing the latent talent of the industrial classes," says Professor Bail of Yale College, "can a people aspire to become a first-class manufacturing nation able to compete successfully with the products of skilled industry in the great markets of the world. . . . The whole nation is deploring the lack of good ornamental designers. We are becoming tired of sending so many millions to Europe for articles that we might produce cheaper at home if we had skilful designers. This branch of industry affects articles for the homeliest use."

"The American mechanic has heretofore been more ingenious than artistic," says Mr. Nichols, author of "Art Education applied to Industry." "His inventive faculty exceeds that of any other people, but he has not had the advantages of artistic training. He has filled the world with useful labor-saving machines, without adding much to the sum of grace and beauty. It has been the tendency of our industries to save labor by making the laborer almost as automatic as the machine itself. If this condition of things is not changed, we shall go on in our subserviency to European art-products, and will never be able to gain any independence or individuality. Art is decidedly practical, and concerns the well-being, the advancement, the pleasure, of the laborer and the poor. How can it be developed? How can it be applied? How can it be put to the best use? The experience of other nations teaches us what we have to do, and how it is to be done. It is by technical education in public and special schools; by the study of great works of art; by the establishment of museums which shall be opened to the public; by the organization of societies in the interest of special industries; by expositions of pictures, statuary, objects of ancient art, and of all products into whose composition art may enter. Art is not the privilege of a class: it is essentially human, and is both individual and universal."

Our country sadly needs institutions like the noble one at South Kensington, richly endowed and liberally fostered, where the people can have a thorough and systematic education in the principles and practice of art. With the amazing growth of our nation's wealth, and the rapid development of a right public sentiment, the private practical movements to insure art-instruction must eventually become universal and national. At the present rate of paying the national debt it will be disposed of in a dozen years. To what nobler use can a portion of the vast revenues of the nation then be devoted, than to the industrial education of its people? giving to its men and women a broad art-culture, which would speedily double their producing power by enabling them to wed art to industry, to add beauty to whatever articles they manufacture. There will always be a fixed limit to the demand for simple, rude manufactures, even in America, — articles of utility only, like shovels, spades, and stoves, ploughs, hammers, and carts. But the demand for articles of beauty, of skilled artistic labor, will be limited only by the cultivated taste to appreciate them, and the ability to purchase.

Since cultivation of art must be bred into a people, and be slowly assimilated by them, it is a matter of congratulation that in so many American cities a movement for industrial-art education has been well begun. A system similar to that at South Kensington has been established in Massachusetts; and its Normal Art-School has graduated large numbers of art-teachers, chiefly

## Industrial and Technical Training. 101

women, the supply not realizing the demand. The Lowell Free School of Industrial Design, connected with the Boston Institute of Technology, also affords to women opportunities of education; and a school of fine arts has recently been added to the Boston Conservatory of Music, an institution patronized by tens of thousands of young women. The Massachusetts State Legislature has made elementary drawing a compulsory subject of instruction in every public school of the State where the population of the town is ten thousand and over that number, and recommending it in all. In addition the city of Boston has provided a normal drawing-school for the teachers of the common schools. The movement for industrial-art education has begun in Massachusetts, where the accumulated capital is largely invested in manufactures under great advantages and very favorable auspices.

In Philadelphia a school of design for women was established in 1853 by the wife of the British consul. It has been greatly stimulated in its growth and usefulness since the Centennial Exposition. Nearly three hundred women students availed themselves of its opportunities during the last year. It teaches architecture, engraving, lithography, and practical design: indeed it would be difficult to indicate a direction in which the artistic skill obtained in this school may not be made available or useful. Many of its graduates are teachers, giving art-instruction; or they are applying what they have learned to manufactures and the common uses of life.

In Cincinnati there is a school of design in which large numbers of women are studying; and in connection with it, or growing out of it, a school of wood-carving has sprung up, which has few superiors in Europe, and here also women are found working and studying. Potteries have been established by Mrs. Nichols, which, in connection with the studios behind them, offer to women excellent opportunities for education in this branch of art. They are the beginning of a school of sculpture worthy the name.

The Women's Art-School at the Cooper Institute in New York does not give general art-education, but is very helpful to women in the instruction it affords in freehand drawing, drawing upon wood, wood-engraving, painting, and similar branches of art. A School of Architecture and Design has also recently been established at the University of Michigan, at which institution

## Industrial and Technical Training. 103

there are about three hundred women students. In the women's colleges, — Vassar, Smith, Wellesley, and others, — as well as in some of the colleges where co-education prevails, there is either a special department in art-education, or lectures on art are given, and collections made. Other schools of design for women have been established in St. Louis, Milwaukee, and other cities, — ten in all; each of them offering to women advantages to acquire a knowledge of art-industries which will give them remunerative occupation.

For the woman who has a thorough art-education can to-day easily find employment. The demand for art-teachers is in excess of the supply. Eighteen young ladies, who graduated this season from a school of design in one of our Eastern cities, found immediate and lucrative employment. Occupation in the useful and ornamental arts will give to the rising ambition and talent of American girls a large and noble scope. "There is an unworked mine of untold wealth among us," says Professor Walter Smith, "in the art-education of women. . . . We could utilize much human life, not now profitably occupied, by educating and employing women as teachers of art. There are also many branches of art workmanship, requiring delicate fingers and native readiness of taste, which could be better performed by women than men." There is, therefore, for our young women, obliged to think of self-support, a large and hopeful future. Industrial art furnishes them with a fitting for many kinds of employment, pleasant and profitable, labor well suited to their tastes, their strength, and capacity. They must be willing to elevate their standard of preparation; must be content to serve a long, and sometimes laborious, apprenticeship to their various professions.

No investment of funds will yield so large an interest to an American city as the money given to found technical and industrial schools, where our gifted and promising girls can be trained for such occupations at small expense to themselves. Their commercial value alone should give them practical importance in any community. And as industrial art and fine art have, in the main, the same elementary basis, whatever promotes the former must aid the latter directly or indirectly; and thus the public taste will be elevated, and the public judgment of art-matters educated.

" The great lesson of history is," says Ruskin, " that all the fine arts hitherto having been sup-

## Industrial and Technical Training. 105

ported by the selfish power of the *noblesse*, and never having extended their range to the comfort and relief of the mass of the people, have only accelerated the ruin of the States they adorned. And at the moment when, in any kingdom, you point to the triumphs of its greatest artists, you point also to the determined hour of the kingdom's decline. The names of great painters are like passing bells. In the name of Velasquez you hear sounded the fall of Spain; in the name of Titian, that of Venice; in the name of Leonardo, that of Milan; in the name of Raphael, that of Rome.

"We may abandon the hope — or, if you like the words better, we may disdain the temptation — of the pomp and grace of Italy in her youth. For us there can be no more the throne of marble, for us no more the vault of gold; but for us there is the loftier and lowlier privilege of bringing the power and charm of art within the reach of the humble and the poor. And, as the magnificence of past ages failed by its narrowness and pride, ours may prevail and continue by its universality and its lowliness.

"We are about to enter upon a period of our world's history in which domestic life, aided by the arts of peace, will slowly, but at last surely and entirely, supersede public life and the arts of war. . . . We want no more feasts of the gods nor martyrdoms of saints. We have no need of sensuality, no place for superstition or for costly insolence. Let us have learned and faithful historical paintings, touching and thoughtful representations of human nature in dramatic painting, poetical and familiar renderings of natural objects and of landscape, and rational, deeply felt realizations of the events which are the subjects of our religious faith. And let these things which we want, as far as possible, be scattered abroad, and made accessible to all men.

"So, also, in manufacture. We require work substantial rather than rich in make, and refined rather than splendid in design. They should be such as may at once serve the need, and refine the taste, of a cottager. It should be one of the first objects of all manufacturers to produce stuffs, not only beautiful and quaint in design, but also adapted for every-day service, and decorous in humble and secluded life."

I have emphasized the need and value of industrial-art education for our young women, because of the deficiency in this respect in our present school-systems; and because it offers to the ambition of women an almost limitless field, not crowded with applicants, as is the profession of teaching. Moreover, the Centennial Exhibition of Industry, held in our country only seven years ago, was most potent in creating dissatisfaction with our present inartistic methods of work. It revealed to the people of the United States how far they were below most European nations in products involving taste, which adds greatly to market-value. It stimulated a hunger and thirst for the knowledge of the harmonies of form, color, and arrangement, which can be used to give beauty to all objects of industry. Americans are not dull nor inapt observers, and they will not long consent to be surpassed by other nations.

And when, in addition, a New-England manufacturer makes the statement that the designs used in his factory "cost forty thousand dollars yearly, every dollar of which goes to England, France, and Germany, and that the same designs might have been made within a mile of his mill for five thousand dollars if an art-school had been maintained there for five years," we have a very strong reason for the conviction that the technical schools and schools of design, already doing such good work, will be increased, and rendered thoroughly efficient. When was an American accused of indifference to any question of money-saving or money-making? The difficulties in the way of art-education vanish daily. Its agencies and its area have doubled in the last half-dozen years, and are already providing employment for large numbers of women.

There are other lucrative employments open to women of which there need be no mention. All are familiar with them. Some industries which have been called "women's work" are now shared by men, who compete with women; and women are working in occupations hitherto considered belonging to men. Men compete with women in the business of cooking, and largely monopolize that occupation in large hotels, fashionable boarding-houses, railway eating-stations, restaurants, steamboats, steamships, and elsewhere; while bakers, caterers, and confectioners are almost universally men. But while doing what is yet called "woman's work" they are not content to accept "woman's pay;" and the president of Harvard College receives a smaller salary than is paid to some men cooks in famous culinary establishments. It is urged that laundry-work belongs to women; but the majority of the washerwomen

## Industrial and Technical Training. 109

whom I have encountered in the country are washer-*men*. Not yet, after twenty years' experience in American travel, have I found a laundry run by women. Laundries there are in plenty, stretching all the way from Mount Katahdin to Santa Barbara; but their proprietors are men universally, who by the aid of labor-saving machinery do vast amounts of work, receiving for it vast amounts of money.

So of millinery and dressmaking. They are always called "women's trades." But if there is a wholesale millinery establishment in the country, kept by women, I have yet to know it. There may be, but diligent inquiry has failed to reveal it to me. When the retail woman milliner goes from the country to the great city, to select her goods for the season, a man milliner receives her, helps her choose her stock, fits her out with pattern hats and bonnets, directs her as to their *bizarre* or graceful decoration, and tells her, — for he knows, as he and his class ordain it, — not only what is worn, but what is to be worn during the season. She returns to her home; and when the women make their *début* on Easter Sunday in hats made as directed, men laugh at the ridiculous guys they have made of themselves, and the papers keep up a running fire of pasquinade to break down the fashion, which, nevertheless, they never accomplish. The handsomest and most costly dresses of women are the work of men, not only in Paris, but in Chicago and in other American cities; one man dressmaker advertising that he "gives undivided personal attention to the trimming of dresses." Indeed no small proportion of "ready-made clothing," both for the wear of men and women, is made by men. One of the philanthropic women of New York, who had personally superintended the training of a large class of dependent girls till they were thoroughly skilled sewing-machine operators, failed to find employment for them. Investigating the cause of this failure, and wondering that there was no market for the skilled labor of these young girls, she found tenement-houses buzzing from basement to attic with the whir of sewing-machines, — three and four in every room, — more than half of them operated by men engaged in the manufacture of "ready-made clothing." We are constantly met with a classification of women's industries, are informed what work is theirs by right of fitness and propriety, what they may do "with safety to themselves and society," and what not.

Col. Higginson tells us of "a school committee, in a Massachusetts town which shall be nameless, who said seriously in their report, speaking of a certain appointment, 'As this place offers neither honor nor profit, we do not see why it should not be filled by a woman.'" Work of this description has been considered woman's work ever since the world began. But a man's work, what is it? It is any work he chooses to perform, in-doors or out-doors, "up-stairs or down-stairs, or in the lady's chamber," by which he can make money. Let us not complain; for we seem to be approximating a condition of things where women will have equal freedom. To-day they are saleswomen, cashiers, bookkeepers, telegraphers, compositors, stenographers, type-writers, watchmakers, chemists, pharmacists, journalists, authors, lecturers, physicians, lawyers, clergywomen, — the list is so long we will not continue it.

Thoroughly educated and duly qualified women physicians are in demand everywhere, and soon find lucrative practice. They are aided by the noblest of the men in the profession, who generously champion their cause, and seek to open to them every door of opportunity that will better furnish them for the work they have undertaken.

And if, here and there, some belated association of men physicians, not yet overtaken by the broadening spirit of the age, refuses them recognition and fellowship, it is a small matter, and does not perceptibly retard the woman physician in her work. State after State wheels into line in the recognition of women lawyers, and in conceding to them the legal right to practise law; and it has been judicially settled that any woman admitted to the bar of her own State may practise in the courts of the United States. Not only are law schools open to women, but the Methodist, Universalist, Unitarian, and Christian denominations receive women into theological schools; and the last three ordain them to the work of the ministry, and install them over parishes.

If there are women desiring to enter into work not yet open to them, and who are conscious of the taste and capacity that entitle them to undertake it, they may be sure of "winning their way," if that is their resolute purpose. To a consecrated, resolute soul, there are no impossibilities. There are, however, inexorable conditions of success, which must be complied with. Only by a thorough fitting for the work to be done, maintaining the standard of preparation at the highest, and then

## Industrial and Technical Training. 113

by a conscientious performance of it afterwards, can women expect to hold the positions already gained, or to enter higher departments of work from which custom now debars them. No favors should be asked or expected on the score of gallantry or because of womanhood. Work takes no account of sex; and our young women must carefully measure their health and strength before aspiring to enter untrodden fields of effort.

I cannot leave this topic of woman's industrial training without speaking of our culpability in neglecting to give our daughters some knowledge of business affairs. With utter indifference on our part they are allowed to grow to womanhood unfamiliar with the most ordinary forms of business transactions, — how to make out bills, and to give receipts; how to draw bank-checks; how to make notes, and what are the cautions to be observed concerning them; what is the best method of transmitting funds to a distance, whether by postal orders or bank-drafts; what are safe rates of interest; how to purchase a life annuity, or effect an insurance on life or property, and so on.

If property is to pass into their possession our daughters certainly need to know much more than this, that they may be able to manage it with wisdom, or even to retain it securely. They need to know what are the elements of financial security; what may be considered safe investments; how to rent, improve, or sell property; what margin of property above the amount of the loan should be required, when it is made on real estate; what constitutes a valid title to property; what cautions are to be observed concerning mortgages; what are the property-rights of married women in the States of their residence, with other like information.

It is rather hazardous to advise wives to anchor their own property securely and legally in their own right; and yet this is, not unfrequently, the wisest course for both husband and wife. For if financial ruin overtake the husband the wife's patrimony remains, usually given her for her own use, — a partial and temporary dependence for both and for their children, while the husband seeks to re-instate himself in business. The interests of a dependent family of young children are altogether too sacred to be jeopardized in the hazards of American business when it is possible to avoid it; and yet there are many wives who would receive such common-sense advice with sentimental scorn. "If I can trust myself with my husband, can I not trust him also with my property?" they loftily inquire; but they cannot always. For a man may be a most excellent husband, — tender, just, appreciative, the very soul of honor and manliness, in his relations with his wife, — and yet be a very poor financier. I have known many such. I think it is Mr. Henry Kidder, the eminent Boston banker, who tells us that "ninety out of every one hundred men fail who go into business;" but I doubt if any one would say that ninety out of every one hundred husbands prove themselves unworthy in the marriage relation. Men who are wise will scorn risking the inheritance of their wives in the fearful fluctuations of the American business-world.

There is one other matter about which there can be but one opinion. The family homestead should be secured to the wife inviolably. She should hold it in fee, secure from the blunders of crazy speculators, who dishonor legitimate business; from the squanderings of the debauchee, who sinks the husband in the sensualist; and from the sad reverses which befall the honest, sore-pressed man of business. Never should the homestead be made the basis for business credit. And the wife should stand firm in the resolve never to consent to the mortgage of the home, nor to its sale, — unless a change of residence compels it, and she is sure that the sale of one home is antecedent to the purchase of another.

Of course there are instances to which this recommendation is not applicable. But to the majority of wives and mothers, filled with tender solicitude for the present and future well-being of their children, there would be infinite comfort and helpfulness in the conviction that they were anchored in permanent homes, while rearing their little ones. For them the terrors of unhoused poverty are unbearable; and the wiser legislation of the future will make the homestead their indefeasible heritage, that they may accomplish the best results for the family. Widowed, if all else has been wrecked, if there remain to the wife an unencumbered home, happiness has not wholly parted company with her. A moderate income can make her comfortable. But if widowed and homeless, she is doubly bereft, is unsettled, and subject to great discomforts.

With a sharp pang that returns as I recall the circumstance I have just seen the friend of many years go out forever from the home which has been the Eden of her married life. At the close of the war, her husband returned to New England from the West, where his business-life had been passed. He brought an ample fortune, and settled in the suburbs of Boston, in a cosey and valuable home. He had been a business-man, and the demon of unrest took possession of him. He was easily lured into a business new to him, with a partner younger than himself, who had had experience, but who risked no capital. Almost from the beginning, there was loss, which continued year after year, with slight interruption, till the comfortable fortune had melted away, like snow in the spring. With a white face, the struggling husband came to his wife, and besought her to consent to mortgage their home, that he might make one more last venture. She knew that this meant homelessness for both in their nearing old age, that no retrieval of his fortunes was possible, and that, if she consented, it would only postpone bankruptcy for a very few days; and she struggled to keep the homestead. For a time, she was firm in her purpose, — and then the home was as heavily mortgaged as the property would allow.

The crash came, and the husband went down with his fallen fortunes. Within a few months, he has died. What remains for the widow? Past middle life, without children, with no relatives or friends able to assume the burden of her support, in broken health, with her former affluence so swept away that she was barely able to pay the expenses of her husband's burial, — she must begin her life anew, face a world which cares little for unfortunate women, and address herself to the ways and means of self-support. Were her home left her, with its convenient suites of rooms, its bit of orchard, its grapery, its vines and roses, she would be neither hopeless nor helpless. When will wives effectually comprehend that the mortgage of the homestead is the very sword of Damocles, suspended over their heads by a single hair?

## CHAPTER VI.

### MORAL AND RELIGIOUS TRAINING.

"But why do you say nothing of the moral and religious education of our daughters?" I am asked. "Do you consider that secondary to their training in other directions?" By no means. And I have been very unfortunate in my utterances if I have given that impression. Moral education should begin with the life of the child. It should be conveyed in the very tones of the mother's voice, in the expression of her face, in the gestures she employs, and in her manner even; all which are felt by a child, harmfully or beneficially, in its earliest moments of consciousness. Moral training underlies and permeates all other training when it is wisely and judiciously given. The education of the will to the customs and habits of good society begins long before the child is old enough to reason on the subject. But its education to the law of right, its submission to the will of God, while it must be begun early, cannot be carried on to perfection, until the child's reason is developed, and its moral nature evolved, sufficiently to feel how paramount to all other demands are those of right and duty.

In the near past it was the custom for clergymen, and those interested in the education of girls, to write books on the subject of their moral and religious education, which undoubtedly were helpful at the time. The market has been overstocked with books of guidance for women and girls, wives, mothers, and maids. Very few of these which survive have any great value to-day. Most of them were vitiated by having been written from the wrong stand-point. Their authors assumed that woman was an accident of creation, called into being only to supplement man, and to answer his needs; whose inferior and adjunct she was thus proclaimed. And the instruction given concerning her moral and religious training was in accordance with this estimate of her status.

But it is no heresy now to teach that God made man and woman two halves of one whole, — equal, but different; and that he created them for the same cause, and to the same ultimate end.

## Moral and Religious Training. 121

They are alike amenable to the laws of God, which are supreme, and to be obeyed in contravention of the laws of man when these conflict. The moral and religious training of our daughters therefore should take cognizance of this change in the enlightened public sentiment. Milton's theory, that man was to be "for God only," but woman for "God through man," is not now accepted: it is heterodox. Both man and woman are to be "for God only." There are not two standards of right and wrong, — one for man, and one for woman. Nor are there two standards of morality. It is as wrong for a man to be intemperate and unchaste as for a woman, no matter what a depraved public sentiment may declare to the contrary. It is as wrong for a woman to live an idle life, to be unveracious, truckling, and dishonorable, as for a man. And this we must teach our daughters thoroughly till it permeates their whole being, — that there is but one law of right for both man and woman, which is supreme, and from which there is no appeal.

The perfectibility of the human being, whether man or woman, is the end to be sought in all training; and that training which helps the child, as it develops into mature life, to yield unquestioning obedience to the law of right, which is the law of God, and to cultivate all human virtues, tends towards that perfection of character, which, begun here, will be continued hereafter, in another life, on a higher plane. Loyalty to right, truth, and duty must be the rule of our lives, personally, as women — and the same is true of men — if we wish to know the highest peace, the completest satisfaction, to live with respect for ourselves, and as helpers of the struggling, straying, sorrowing world. This is the law of personal life we must teach our children, — sons and daughters, — steadily, by precept and example, in season and out of season.

Nor must this law of life, inexorable and supreme, ever be set aside, to accommodate or please or aid others. We owe obedience to God, to right, truth, and duty; and we are also held to the observance of social duties. But the first — the law of God — can never be ignored or abrogated, because of any duty we owe our fellow-beings. Frances Power Cobbe, in her recent and unequalled book, "Duties of Women," makes this very clear. I quote from its pages: —

"I hold that, whenever personal and social duties seem to come into collision, personal duty must have the precedence. We must not sacrifice our veracity or chastity or temperance, in the vain hope of benefiting our neighbors, for these two plain reasons. First, because virtue is the true end of our being, and we can only choose virtue for ourselves, and not for another. We can *never* make anybody else virtuous, — only, in an indirect way, *help* him to virtue; and so it follows that it is absurd to postpone our own virtue to any lesser object.

"And, secondly, because we can never really benefit anybody by doing wrong on his behalf; and the truest and surest way in which we can serve our fellow-men is not so much to *do* any thing for them, as to *be* the very purest, truest, noblest beings we know how. This is, I fear, a hard lesson to take to heart. And you will pardon me, if, in addressing women, I dwell on it specially, because I think it is a matter on which the most generous-hearted women are most apt to err.

"There have been hundreds of women, who, like Judith of old, or like the piteous, poverty-stricken mother in 'Les Miserables,' will sacrifice their chastity to serve their race or their children. There are thousands, tens of thousands, of women, who, like the wife of 'Auld Robin Gray,' have made unloving marriages — which are in truth, though not in name, unchaste likewise — to aid their parents in distress, and even to gratify their wishes. And, again, there are thousands of women — and of men also — who are ready to sacrifice their veracity to do charitable actions; to conceal some one's faults, that they may be helped to employment; and, in short, to bear false witness *for* their neighbors, — the reverse of the noble and sweet examples of Jeannie Deans and Mary Barton.

"It is a mere truism, but at the same time a profound truth, to say, 'It can never be right to do wrong.' It is not even right to *suffer* one kind of wrong, — that is, the wrong which robs us of our sacred birthright of moral freedom. . . . It is *the living man or woman*, himself or herself, which lifts us up, or drags us down, and in whose 'sphere' — as the Swedenborgians say — we are elevated and purified, or polluted and degraded; made nobler and larger by the one, or belittled by the other. All the greatest saints and heroes and prophets of history have influenced mankind far more by what they *were*, than by what they said or did. The whole moral life of the farther East has been colored by the mind and heart of Gautama Buddha. And the stupendous change which has passed over humanity during the last eighteen hundred years, and which we name Christianity, has had for its mainspring, acting to this hour through millions of hearts, not so much the Sermon on the Mount, or even the martyrdom of Calvary, as the personal character of Jesus Christ."

But we have not only personal, but social duties. We owe it to ourselves to be so faithful and true in living, that we shall be uplifted to a divine altitude of spiritual power and vision; but we also owe love and helpfulness, not alone to our kindred and friends, but to the human race. The desolation of the world when it was ignorant of the great fundamental law of justice and charity, which, with appreciative speech, we call "the Golden Rule," may be read in the pages of history. Brute force ruled. War was the normal business of nations. Cruelty and slavery, tyranny and savagery, have wrought such immitigable woe in the past, among all peoples, that it can neither be measured nor comprehended. Neither earthquake nor pestilence, famine nor flood, tempest nor wild beast, has been to man the most destructive foe. Man, in his ravages of cruelty and brutality, has scourged his race more than they all united.

As out of the chaos of creation there was slowly evolved the green earth, so out of the stormy past, red with war, and lurid with brutal passion, there has been slowly developed the divine law, "Do unto others as you would have them do to you." While Confucius uttered it as a negation, and Plato breathed it as a prayer, Christ announced it as a law of life. He did more: he interpreted it by a life of such wonderful love and benevolence, that it took root in the heart of the world, and is now slowly coming to fruition. Taught to measure another's rights and sufferings by his own man has gradually taken on increasing fineness and tenderness, and civilization has become more humane and just. One needs to possess "the cultivated attributes of manhood" to feel the demands of "the Golden Rule," or to be successfully governed by it. But the growth of civilization, and the binding authority of this law, have kept pace with each other; and it is recognized to-day as the divinest regulator of our social life.

It is still ignored by that aggregate of individuals which we call nations, and national life is still largely under the dominion of brute force. But this will not be forever; for the day draws near when this simple rule, the panacea for so many of the ills of life, will constitute the indwelling spirit of kingdoms and republics.

Let our daughters, then, be early trained, not only to yield unquestioning obedience to the behests of right and duty, but also to know, practically, the divine happiness that comes from self-renunciation. Teach them by experience the blessedness that comes from deeds done for others, the farthest removed from selfish considerations. Let them learn that the periods of our lives which give us most joy at the moment, and which are most exquisite in memory, are those when we have gone the most wholly out of ourselves, and lived for others. She who seeks excellence, and not reputation alone, rises highest in her pursuits; and she who foregoes her own pleasures, — ignoring, it may be, her own rights, — and forgets herself, in her genuine interest for others, attains to the surest and most satisfactory enjoyment. The secret of many low and miserable lives is the complete absorption of the man and the woman in their own pleasures and wants, cares, character, and prospects.

All the names of the past that the world holds dear and sacred are those who have renounced self that they might seek the happiness and well-being of others. Howard, Wilberforce, Washington, Lincoln, Garrison, Florence Nightingale, Elizabeth Fry, Ann Hasseltine Judson, Mary Carpenter, Mary Lyon, the Sisters of Charity and Mercy, — all these, and others of the same noble and unselfish order, are held tenderly in the thought of millions. "The world can do without its masters better than it can without its servants," said Dr. S. G. Howe, himself one of its most untiring servants, always ready to answer the call of its most unfortunate classes, the law of whose grand life was service to the world.

Whoever is a lover of the race will not be content to look on supinely and in indifference while sin and crime, injustice and oppression, flourish and grow rampant about him. To shut ourselves in convents and monasteries, as did the saints of mediæval times; or to stand aloof from the world on an imaginary pinnacle of fastidious culture and æsthetic refinement, as is the tendency of our day, holding away our garments from its grossness and wrong-doing as if the touch were pollution, — this is to be guilty of weakness and cowardice, or to be wickedly selfish. The world has progressed because an advance guard of noble men and women in all ages have led the way to a higher civilization. In the face of the rack and gibbet and headman's axe they have condemned the low and brutal ideas and practices of their time, and have compelled the world to uplift its vision to a higher ideal.

Some one has said, "A religion in which one good man will become ten good men is the only one that will offer society hope." That is the religion in which we should train not only our daughters, but our sons: so that, standing in the midst of evil, they will not run from it, nor ally themselves with it; but maintaining their own integrity, and protesting against the wrong, they will draw the erring up to their standard through the might of their earnestness, and the divine attraction of their excellent lives.

To love God, and to love one's neighbor, are the cardinal doctrines of Christianity. Let them be taught our children in the home practically and earnestly. Neither the training of the heart nor the hand can be given over to the public school. Scanty place is found there as yet for either branch of education. How to fashion character, how to give ethical training, how to develop the religious nature, how to rear our daughters to be living influences for the good and true, — these are problems for mothers to solve; for to them is committed in large measure the responsibility of the work. Let our children be taught that they are children of God, so divine in ancestry, so royal of parentage, that they must carry themselves nobly, and not consent to meanness, low, selfish lives, and vice. Let us teach them that to love God is to love whatever is good and just and true; and that loving brothers, sisters, schoolmates, and humanity as a whole, are also loving God, since God is our common Father, and "we are all brethren."

Let us seek to train children to regard earthly life as the first school of the soul, where there are lessons to be learned, tasks to be mastered, hardships to be borne, and where God's divinest agent of help is often hindrance; and that only as we learn well the lessons given us here, may we expect to go joyfully forward to that higher school to which we shall be promoted, where the tasks will be nobler, the lessons grander, the outlook broader, and where life will be on a loftier plane. While the coldness of scepticism seems to be creeping over the age, — mainly, I believe, because of its great immersion in materialism of life and activity, — it is possible to train children to such far-reaching, telescopic religious vision that they will overlook all fogs and mists of doubt. The low fears and dismaying presages that weigh down so many souls will be dispelled by the clear atmosphere in which they will dwell; and with hearts throbbing evenly with the heart of God they will say confidently, "Because He lives, I shall live also."

## CHAPTER VII.

### SUPERFLUOUS WOMEN.

To all the arguments for woman's better industrial training, and to all the movements now in progress for its accomplishment, there is constantly interposed the objection that it interferes with the marriage of women. The objection definitely stated is this: that if women are trained to self-support, and are able to maintain themselves by their own labor, they will not marry, but will ignore their "fore-ordained work as mothers and nurses of children."

Dr. Ely Van de Warker, in "The Popular Science Monthly," avers that "the effort of woman to invade all the higher forms of labor is a force battling with the established order of sexual relation."

Dr. Nathan Allen of Lowell, Mass., in "The Journal of Psychological Medicine," says, "In all the situations and pursuits of life the Almighty has established bounds, or limitations, beyond which woman cannot go without defeating the primary objects of her creation; and maternity is the primary law of her creation."

Charles W. Eliot, writing in the August number of "The North-American Review," 1882, says, "Girls are being prepared daily, by 'superior education,' to engage, not in child-bearing and house-work, but in clerkships, telegraphy, newspaper-writing, school-teaching, etc. And many are learning to believe, that, if they can but have their 'rights,' they will be enabled to compete with men at the bar, in the pulpit, the Senate, the bench."

Now, women have done most of the drudgery of the world since it was peopled. They are to-day doing much of its menial labor, of which men are glad to be rid. Everywhere in Continental Europe you see women engaged in the most laborious and servile work. I have seen them unloading freight-cars at the railroad stations; mixing mortar, making brick; quarrying stone, and hewing it; building the road-beds of railways; sawing and splitting wood, and then mounting with it on their backs up four and six flights of stairs, where they packed it away snugly in back-closets; climbing to the top of six and seven story buildings on ladders, bearing hods of brick and mortar for the convenience of masons; drawing ploughs through the furrow, while other women guided them; bent under heavy loads, borne on their backs in baskets graded to carry sixty pounds; harnessed with dogs, goats, cows, mules, and donkeys, and drawing heavy cart-loads, — in short, there is no imaginable drudgery, or servility of labor, into which women are not forced on the continent of Europe.

You do not wholly escape such sights in Christian Britain, nor indeed in America. In my own country I have seen women sawing and splitting wood; on their hands and knees, hours before daylight, scrubbing the floors and stairs of offices, in hotels, and public buildings; staggering under loads, sometimes of fuel, and sometimes of material to be worked up at home; sometimes, amid coal and iron manufactures, shovelling coke and coal into freight-cars, and doing other like hard manual work, to which, indeed, in many instances, they seemed adapted physically. Where the wife and mother performs all the household labor for a family of four, six, or more persons, — husband and children, — cooking, washing, ironing, making, mending, nursing the sick, and caring for the house, she is compelled to labor very severely. And this is the condition of the majority of the married women of America. Dr. E. H. Clarke, author of "Sex in Education," declares that "the duties of the mother of a family require as much toil of brain and body as those of a captain of a ship."

I do not complain that women must toil, and toil severely. Greater harm befalls them in indolence than is encountered in severe, honest industry. I only ask that they shall have a physical and industrial training that shall lighten severe labor, and give them fair remuneration. But this is the point. Magazine-articles and pamphlets and books were never written to complain that woman is compelled to work; nor to trumpet an alarm concerning the terrible dangers this work will inflict on her prospective maternity, until, as Van de Warker announces, she began "to invade all the higher forms of labor," or as Eliot expresses it in clumsy phraseology, "to prepare, by superior education, to engage in clerkships, telegraphy, newspaper-writing, school-teaching, etc." The gravamen of these accusations is, that woman "labors for bread in the same field with man." It is, seemingly, "the superior education," "the higher forms of labor," and the equality of work that have caused the amazing scientific and literary affliction of the day, which is calling upon the world for condolence. Women have always been toilers from a time coincident with the beginning of history, and, undoubtedly, anterior to that; but no tears have been shed for them, save what they have wept themselves, until they began to enter higher fields of labor, and to receive better compensation. Lo! then the floodgates of grief are hoisted, and there is mourning that will not be comforted.

Nor are women refusing to marry, or "remaining unmarried," because "they are now able to support themselves;" nor yet, as Eliot asserts in "The North-American Review," because they are the victims of "impracticable theories," expecting "to become the idols of men, and to receive every thing, and to do nothing," "to be helped, and not to be helpful;" nor yet because, according to the same authority, "not one woman in ten is a fairly healthy creature;" nor because, being "sick in body," "women are sensitive, nervous, possibly fretful and unhappy." If all these criticisms of women are just, and if every charge is proved true, they tell very little on marriage.

For women do marry, and are marrying continually. The young people of the community in which I live are wedded about as soon as they reach the marriageable age; one couple going to Dakota, another to Colorado, another to some neighboring city or remaining in the town, according to their plans for a future home. I see that women who earn large incomes marry,— women like Christine Nilsson and Annie Cary,— actresses, prime donne, vocalists, women principals of academies and normal schools, women physicians, women lawyers, clergywomen, women authors, women journalists, etc.

There is a vast deal of nonsense written and talked on this subject. Human beings are born to marry, as they are born to die. Nature has overloaded men and women with the instinct that leads to marriage, that the race may be perpetuated; and at the proper age the young man turns to the young woman, as she also turns to him with love in their hearts, and vague visions of husbandhood and wifehood, fatherhood and motherhood, flitting through their souls. "The widespread neglect, indifference, or opposition to marriage," discussed and anathematized by some late writers, exists more generally in their imaginations than in society. For to-day, as ever since the world began, men and women marry, wisely and unwisely, the healthy and the diseased, the rich and the poor, the brutal and the refined, men and women of all classes and of all ages. And the results are the same as they have ever been, — children sufficient to keep the world a-going, good, bad, and indifferent; wretchedness, so supreme, that it beggars description; happiness, so divine, as to make of earth an elysium; and a medium condition, where is content or indifference.

It is true there are communities where women are in excess of men, as in Massachusetts where they outnumber men by more than sixty thousand. The exhortation of Horace Greeley, "Go West, young man, go West!" has been largely heeded by the young men of the Eastern States, mainly those most enterprising and energetic. They have emigrated in such numbers, that while there is in the whole country, according to the United-States census, an excess of men, there are large communities in the East where there is an excess of women. It is very evident in such communities that there will be large numbers of unmarried women, unless the surplusage of women should emigrate, — Heaven only knows where, — or Utah be re-enacted in New England. The laws forbid the latter, if it were not forbidden by a high civilization. And the women, who have a right to decide concerning the former, very naturally choose to remain among their friends and kindred. No theory therefore is necessary to account for the non-marriage of tens of thousands of Eastern women. The facts explain it. And these same facts form an imperative reason why "superior education," and "higher forms of labor," should be conceded to them, as also every other needed aid; for they are to be self-dependent and self-supported.

It is also true that the better class of women, the more thoughtful and the more refined, demand more in marriage at the present time than was formerly thought essential. Not more in the way of worship or luxury or indolence; but the theory of the wife's equality with the husband has rooted itself in the minds of most women; and the old-time doctrine of marital domination and wifely submission still has zealous advocates among men. "Suppose woman finds too late, that she is doomed (in marriage) to walk with a soulless brute, then what? Let her soberly accept her lot." This was the advice given by a doctor of divinity five or six years ago to the graduating class of Packer Institute, Brooklyn, N.Y. He assumed that the young ladies then graduating were all bound to the marriage altar, that their marriage was inevitable; and he proceeded to teach them that their "lot" was "wifely submission under all circumstances." This may be good advice for a doctor of divinity to give, but it is very poor advice for a woman to follow; and only a minority of a minority will follow it, in our republic, in this age of the world.

Eliot, in an article in "The North-American Review," to which I have before alluded, informs his readers, that "the average man is often ignorant, rough, greedy, sensual. His coarser pleasures and wants consume his earnings. His tastes are vitiated, and the dull serenity of home-life too often seems undesirable." If this is the character of the "average man," then he is unfit for husbandhood and fatherhood. If this pen-picture is a caricature or a libel, let it be remembered that it was drawn, not by a woman, but by a man. From institutes of heredity and temperance unions, from maternal associations and societies for moral education, from press and pulpit, from the heart of the mother, and the experience of the father, — there comes a united entreaty to the young women of the present, to forbear allying themselves in marriage with drunken, sensual, immoral men.

No woman has a moral right to become the mother of children when the father is drunken and immoral. For this perpetuates the brutishness and woe of the race, and gives an extension of time to evils which humanity should outgrow. Unthinking as to their cause, it has appealed to Heaven for relief; throwing itself

> "On the world's great altar-stairs,
> That slope through darkness up to God."

It is learning to-day that relief can only come from obedience to the laws of being, — physical, mental, and moral, — from a higher ideal of marriage, from nobler conditions of parentage. "To give life to a sentient being," says Gail Hamilton, "without being able to make provision to turn life to the best account; to give life, careless whether it will be bale or boon to its recipient, — is the sin of sins. Every other sin mars what it finds: this makes what it mars."

If, therefore, according to the indictment of Dr.

Nathan Allen, "the family life of the New Englander occurs more rarely, begins later in life, and is blessed with fewer offspring," it is because of certain conditions which are mainly indigenous to New England. In the United States as a whole the overwhelming majority of women are wives and mothers; only a very meagre minority remaining outside of married life. As the country advances in age, unless the type of civilization prevailing here shall continue in advance of that of Europe, it will undoubtedly be otherwise. For the same destructive and demoralizing forces will produce here, as there, a great host of women, insulted by the sociologists of the day with the epithet "*superfluous*," because, forsooth, they are in excess of men in numbers, and, therefore, cannot marry.

There are a million and a half of unmarried women in Prussia. In Baden thirty-five per cent of women earn their own living. Mr. Bloomfield tells us, in his work on "Brittany," that "it is poverty that fills the convents of the country, not religion." A poor man has a large family of daughters; and, as marriage without fortune is less easy in France than in England, he places them in the convent, and they are cared for during life. The same is true of Italy, where it is not denied by the people that one use of convents is to provide for "superfluous daughters." There is not a nation of Europe in which women do not out-number men. In England and Wales forty-three out of every one hundred women, of the age of twenty and upwards, are unmarried. The census of 1860 gave three and a half millions of women in England working for a subsistence, of whom two and a half millions were unmarried.

In Europe, therefore, there is an absolute necessity that women shall have the largest and most varied industrial training; nor, in view of the facts, would one suppose there would be opposition to this. And yet European "congresses of working-men" manifest hostility that is surprising to the opening of trades or industries to women. One held at Lausanne, Switzerland, declared, "that all moral, physical, and economic arguments are against the employment of women as agents of production." It is a phase of the same narrowness that in America vents its spleen against woman entering "higher forms of labor," and demanding "superior education to engage in clerkships, etc." But in Europe, as in America, the wisest, fairest, and noblest men counteract this small injustice by the scope of their utterances on the other side.

One of the most striking of these was the rectorial address of Professor von Scheel, of the University of Berne, who, a year or two since, urged the necessity of "opening to women all the fresh spheres of activity possible." He attributed the decline of marriage in Europe to the fact that "a woman is less able than formerly to help her husband on account of the extent to which corporate manufacture has superseded domestic industry. Hence to exclude women from any profession or trade for which they prove themselves qualified is to inflict serious injury upon society. Their sex," says this wise professor, "should not constitute an element in the calculation. By a strict adherence to this principle the state has twice as many chances of being efficiently served."

### CAUSES OF A SURPLUS OF WOMEN.

What are the causes underlying this great surplus of women in Europe? It is not, as some declare, because more female than male infants are born into the world. The statistics of the world prove that the reverse is true; that, taking one year with another, there are one hundred and six boys born annually to every one hundred girls. But there is great loss of manly life through the desolating wars of Europe now and heretofore. Drunkenness, and other ruinous excesses peculiar to men, have also depleted their ranks; and the decimation still continues. Emigration thins their numbers, as well as a tendency to rove about the world. While among all civilized nations great fatalities attend the pursuits of men in pleasure or business. The elemental forces of nature are now harnessed in workshops, factories, foundries, mines, steamships, and railways; and, when the laws controlling them are violated, there come inevitable casualties, often resulting in large destruction of men.

War is responsible for a frightful depletion of the ranks of men now and ever. The wars of the world have swept men away by countless millions. The histories of the world which have come down to us have been mainly histories of wars and warrior-kings. "The whole history of the world," says Niebuhr, "turns on war and conquest." There is something appalling in the tendency of the race to rush into war, and in the ferocity and savagery which war develops.

When you utter the one word " war " you have condensed into one monosyllable every thing infernal.

Twelve millions of Romans fell in the Western campaigns of Cæsar, while as many more were slaughtered of those with whom they fought. Four millions of Frenchmen, with their allies, fell in the wars waged by the world-striding, ambitious Napoleon the First. From the eighth to the fifteenth century — a period of seven hundred years — the followers of Mohammed deluged with blood the fairest portions of Christian Europe and of Asia. They fell in millions by the sword of their enemies, of whom they, in return, slaughtered other millions. In less than eight hundred years England, our mother-country, had twenty-four wars with France, one of her nearest neighbors, which occupied two hundred and sixty-six years. In the same time she had twelve wars with Scotland, and eight with Spain. During these nearly eight hundred years she was at war with some nation almost seven hundred years, having only one hundred years of peace. Edmund Burke estimates the number of men destroyed, from the beginning of authentic history to his own time, to have been "*thirty-five thousand millions.*"

To-day the armed peace of Europe is keeping between five and six millions of men in camp under drill, and in readiness for war. One-sixth of its manliest strength and beauty — for soldiers are carefully selected, are "picked men" — is withdrawn from all productive industries, and largely from domestic life; while, as consumers of food and clothing, they require for their support the labor of nearly as many more. Their places are taken by women, who till the ground and build railroads, become mechanics and market-women, beasts of burden and human machines. Thrust into employments unsuited to them, deprived of domestic life, they become de-womanized, almost de-humanized; and endure such loss, — spiritually, mentally, and physically, — that the age suffers through the destruction of the finest qualities of humanity. The aggregated war-debt of Europe is over twenty thousand million dollars, and the annual interest on this debt is almost a thousand million more. The nations owing this money have nothing to show for it, and the industry of millions of laboring people is taxed to pay it.

The evil of strong drink, which has afflicted the world from the beginning, still further depletes the ranks of marriageable men. While it is possible to make an approximate statement of the loss of life by war it is not possible to give the statistics of death occasioned by drinking-habits; but the popular belief is expressed in the well-known saying, "The sword hath slain its millions, but strong drink its tens of millions." Charles Buxton, M.P., the English brewer, declares, that, if we "add together all the miseries generated in our times by war, famine, and pestilence,— the three great scourges of mankind,— they do not exceed those that spring from this one calamity of drink." Rev. H. R. Haweis, incumbent of St. James, Marylebone, London, in an essay on "Drunkenness," recently published, estimates the dipsomaniacs of England, Scotland, and Ireland at six hundred thousand. When we take the calculations of Dr. Willard Parker of New York — who shows from statistics that, for every ten temperate persons who die between the ages of twenty-one and thirty, fifty-one intemperate persons die, so that the mortality of liquor-users is *five hundred per cent greater* than that of temperate persons — we arrive at a vague idea of the deaths caused by drunkenness, not only in the United Kingdom of Great Britain, but in the United States.

According to the calculations of life-insurance experts the expectancy for life of a temperate person at the age of twenty years is forty-four years. The expectancy of an intemperate person at the same age is only fifteen years. A few English life-insurance companies have a separate section for total abstainers, and refuse all who are more than "careful drinkers;" and their statistics show that any use of intoxicating liquors tends to shorten life. It is estimated that between sixty and one hundred thousand persons die annually from the effects of strong drink, not only in Great Britain, but also in America. In the latter country this mortality is chiefly among men, — mainly young men; but in Britain there is more drunkenness among women than is found in our country. Among all Anglo-Saxon or Teutonic nations the evil of drunkenness prevails to a frightful extent. It is no less an evil in Russia; and one needs but little experience among Latin races to be convinced that they are not exempt from the desolating vice, which thins the ranks of men, destroys health, and vitiates manhood. If it were possible to obtain the statistics of drunkenness, we should see that its draughts on the male population exceed those made by war. For while there are periods of time exempt from the ravages of war those caused by drunkenness continue through times of war and times of peace.

The emigration from Europe to the United States, which is one of the amazing phenomena of the times, has attained vast proportions. The great host of newcomers to our shores during the last year numbered nearly a million. Observing how many young men are included in each arrival, who have come without families of their own, it is not difficult to account for the excess of men over women in the West, nor to understand that this steady efflux from Europe increases there the surplus of marriageable women. Add to this the loss of manly lives occasioned by disaster in mines, collieries, storms at sea; and the thousand and one accidents that occur in traffic, labor, business, and travel; the fatalities attending residence in unhealthy climates, and pursuit of occupations fraught with danger, or engendering disease, — and it is easy to understand the decrease of men in Europe, and the increase of women.

Men are willing to incur almost any risk in quest of wealth. Considerations of life and health avail little when balanced against acquisition of property. Wendell Phillips declares, that, "if there were a bomb mortar capable of shooting men across the Atlantic into the streets of Liverpool, and if it were certain that every man shot out alive would immediately be made a millionnaire, but that only one in twenty thousand could make the transit safely, there would be miles of Americans standing in line behind the mortar, each ready to take the risk, sure that he would be the lucky twenty-thousandth that would secure the coveted prize." And it is a pretty fair hit at the risks American men are always willing to take when wealth is the object to be gained. This tendency still further depletes the ranks of marriageable men.

War and drunkenness, however, are the two agents most successful in reducing the male population. To these, more than to all other causes combined, is owing the excess of the marriageable women of the Old World; while the New World is by no means unacquainted with their destructive potency. I confess that I am always amazed at the indifference of women to these two great sources of evil, — sources, also, of immeasurable woe to them. I have an acquaintance with many unmarried women both in Europe and my own country; and among them are some of the grandest women the world has ever seen, living in homes of their own, of the most exalted character, mentally and morally, sources of strength and comfort to all within the circle of their influence. Never yet have I heard an unmarried woman deny that marriage is better for both sexes than celibacy, if it can be effected on the right basis, between proper contracting parties, and under favorable conditions. Happily and rightly married, both men and women attain a more harmonious development, their blessedness is increased, their risks and sorrows are divided, or fade away before the lofty courage born of such a union. When little children enter such a home with encircling arms about the neck, and clinging hands in the hearts of the parents, they incite to nobler living, they broaden the affections, till they are world-wide in their embrace. "Infancy is the perpetual Messiah," says Emerson.

But such marriage is not possible to a very large minority of women while the hideous business called "war" is recognized as the prerogative of nations, and the debasing vice called "drunkenness" is excused and palliated in men. I wonder that the women of the civilized world do not band themselves in perpetual protest against both, taking active measures to develop a public sentiment that shall substitute international arbitration for one, and total abstinence from intoxicating drinks for the other. This is the right, as well as the duty, of women. For they cannot longer afford to go down into the valley of the shadow of death, and win their sons at the risk of their own lives; rearing them afterwards at the sacrifice of all other pursuits, at the cost of their own youth, beauty, and health; and then, when their costliness and worth surpass estimate, yield them as food to insatiate war, or to be drowned in the sluice-ways of drunkenness.

NOT A NEW FEATURE OF CIVILIZATION.

An excess of unmarried women is not, however, as many believe, a new and distinguishing feature of our modern, complicated civilization. An investigation reveals the fact that it was a feature of older and other times. It is doubtful if the number of women who remain outside of wedlock at the present time in England, where the number is largest, exceeds the spinsters of feudal England, taking into account the men and the populations of both ages. The number of women in mediæval England, who never found careers of usefulness as wives and mothers, was very large, without including the large number of gentle birth who were consecrated from the cradle to religious celibacy. "When due allowance has been made for children under education, and ladies under no vow of celibacy, the majority of the gentlewoman-kind, housed in the nunneries of feudal England, consisted of women who never married."

"Life-long celibacy was also the lot of a large part of the well-born and honorably taught women who found their livelihood and employments in castles and manorial halls as serving-women. Hundreds of them to the last earned board and wages as needlewomen, lace-makers, cooks, laundry-women, and housemaids, in days when domestic labor was not thought despicable. And a poor squire's or knight's daughter earning her subsistence in a gentle household in any of the above-named capacities was as creditably placed as the well-born, fashionable governess of Victorian England. In mediæval England the priest was, with only a few exceptions to the rule, wifeless. The regular clergy, who held, and spent chiefly on themselves, the revenues and fruits of a prodigious portion of the real estate of the country, never married. The same may be said of the wealthier ecclesiastics of the secular ranks. The few seculars who, in defiance of canons and bishops, perpetrated furtive wedlock with plebeian women, contributed nothing to the matrimonial chances of girls in the higher social grades."

The great difference between the unmarried women of old and of modern England appears to consist in this: The former were resigned to whatever fate came to them, and submissively endured any treatment meted out to them. Like the masses of men at that day, they were incapable of asserting themselves, and probably had no desire to do so. But the unmarried women of modern civilization, like their brothers, have grown into a noble conception of existence; and, with fuller knowledge, demand justice, and a sphere of activity that shall conduce to their happiness and usefulness.

The holiness of a celibate life has always been warmly encouraged by the Catholic Church. Monasteries were organized early in the second century; and at the end of the third, and the beginning of the fourth century, monachism had taken a definite shape, and monasteries had spread through the Eastern Church with amazing rapidity. To most of the religious orders of men organized in the Catholic Church, soon after their formation, nuns of the same rule, and frequently of the same name, attached themselves. Besides the nuns there were numerous additions to the convents of "lay sisters," who were charged with the performance of the housework, and with keeping up communication. All took the vow of celibacy. In a semi-barbaric age these monasteries and convents were needed as a refuge from the lawlessness of brute force. They became centres of learning, and nurseries of civilization. And, while there is no doubt that great abuses crept into them, and that at times when all the outside world was corrupt, they also dropped into great debasement, they yet prevented much more misery than they ever inflicted.

For nearly sixteen hundred years these religious orders of celibate women have existed, invading every department of the world's work and charity; assuaging the sufferings of millions; diminishing, in places, the vast total of human wretchedness; and developing some of the very noblest types of womanhood. The convent has been open to rich and poor alike; and this, in wild and rough times, when anarchy prevailed, was no doubtful blessing. Whoever among women did not and could not marry was sure of an honored and secure asylum within its walls. If we condemn, in the conventual system, its vows of perpetual celibacy and servitude, it is well to remember, that, if it brought many evils, it also brought many compensations. For to be unmarried, under vows of life-long celibacy, was to be "the spouse of Christ," — a member of a sisterhood surrounded with all the honor and sanctity of the Church. I can well understand how these retreats have furnished much happiness to the tens of thousands of unmarried women, who in all ages have sought them. In the exercises of a religion whose forms satisfied them, and whose teachings nourished them; in their abundant employment, in deeds of charity, in the education of children, in nursing the sick; and in the friendships they formed with one another, — their lives could not have been altogether dreary.

How large a proportion of the women of the last sixteen hundred years have been religiously vowed to celibacy may be vaguely inferred from the fact, that, during the pontificate of Pius IX., when a census of monastic institutions throughout the world was taken, there were ninety-four female orders and congregations, with nine thousand two hundred and forty-seven convents, and a little more than one hundred thousand nuns.

"Catholicism commonly softens, while Protestantism strengthens the character," says Lecky; "but the softness of the first often degenerates into weakness, and the strength of the second into hardness. The complete suppression of the conventual system was very far from a benefit to woman or to the world. It would be impossible to conceive any institution more needed than one which would furnish a shelter for the many women who, from poverty or domestic unhappiness, or other causes, find themselves cast alone and unprotected into the battle of life; which would secure them from the temptations to gross vice, and from the extremities of suffering, and would convert them into agents of active, organized, and intelligent charity. . . . There is," he continues, "no fact in modern history more deeply to be deplored than that the Protestant reformers, who, in matters of doctrinal innovation, were often so timid, should have levelled to the dust — instead of attempting to regenerate — the whole conventual system of Catholicism."

Luther, on several occasions, expressed his approbation of religious communities of men and of women. Solitary voices among the Protestant theologians of the sixteenth, seventeenth, and eighteenth centuries have, with Lecky, expressed regret that the principle of forming communities of men and women for the more efficient fulfilment of the duties of charity has been altogether discarded. Of late, attempts have been made to rebuild the conventual institution. In the English Church, and the Protestant-Episcopal Church in the United States, sisterhoods have been formed at various times under the auspices of what is commonly called "the High-Church party." Since the beginning of the nineteenth century both the "Evangelical" and the "High-Lutheran" schools of Germany have approved the establishment of houses of deacons and deaconesses, the inmates of which associate for the purpose of teaching, of attending the sick, of taking charge of public prisons, and for other works of Christian charity. Institutions of this kind are rapidly spreading in Germany and the adjacent countries. If, with the increasing years of our country, there comes also a large increase of its unmarried women, as has occurred among other civilized nations, there may ensue a re-habilitation of the conventual system, with an excision of its objectionable features, and such additions as shall harmonize with republican institutions. The movement may originate with women, who, with larger education, have developed great ability in associated effort. Their various organizations, formed for many noble purposes, are proving successful everywhere in America, and include women in their memberships by the ten thousand.

### CELIBACY NOT ORIGINAL WITH THE CATHOLIC CHURCH.

But the celibate life, and the conventual system based upon it, did not originate with the Catholic Church. It may be traced through the most distant ages, and through the most varied religions. "We find it," says Lecky, "among the Nazarenes, and Essenes of Judea; among the priests of Egypt and India; in the monasteries of Tartary; and in the histories of miraculous virgins, so numerous in the mythologies of Asia. . . . In the midst of the sensuality of ancient Greece chastity was the pre-eminent attribute of sanctity ascribed to Athene and Artemis. . . . The Parthenon, or virgins' temple, was the noblest religious edifice of Athens. Celibacy was an essential condition in a few of the orders of priests, and in several orders of priestesses. . . . The whole school of Pythagoras made chastity one of its leading virtues, and even labored for the creation of a monastic system. . . . Strabo mentions the existence in Thrace of societies of men and of women aspiring to perfection by celibacy."

The vestal virgins of Rome, to whom intense sanctity was attributed because of their celibacy, readily furnished the hint for the consecration of nuns, and the foundation of convents; while the old fraternities of Pagan priests, like the Augurs and Pontifices, who lived apart from the world, near to the temple of the deity to whose service they were devoted, undoubtedly gave the suggestion for the various societies or orders of Catholic priests. Among the religious orders of ancient pagan Rome there were mendicant priests, corresponding to the begging friars one meets everywhere in Italy, who went from house to house with a sack, begging for the support of their fraternity.

Neither did Greece nor Rome originate the conventual system, with its orders of celibate priests and priestesses. We go farther back to India and Egypt, and find them flourishing there fifteen and twenty centuries before Christ. The human mind repeats its experience age after age. Herodotus tells us that "the names of almost all the gods came from Egypt into Greece;" and adds, that the Greeks learned their religious ceremonial from the Egyptians, who were "beyond measure scrupulous in matters of religion." Five hundred years before Christ the Buddhists had nunneries for women, who took the same vows of chastity, poverty, and obedience as the monks; and these still flourish in India and Thibet. No religion of the Orient is so liberal and fair to woman as Buddhism. Yet more remote in the past we find orders of unmarried priestesses in Egypt, where at one time, it is recorded, there were seventy-six thousand celibate priests, and twenty-seven thousand celibate priestesses.

Superfluous women, therefore, — superfluous in the modern acceptation of the word, because they are unmarried, or in excess of the men who seek wives, — have always existed. History, in its earliest records, makes honorable mention of them as ministers of religion and charity. Almost every one of the great religions of the world has made special provision for them, and the woman who has preferred a celibate to a domestic life has been able to occupy a position of honor and usefulness. With Protestantism it has been otherwise. "Puritanism is the most masculine form that Christianity has yet assumed," says Lecky. It has purified and dignified marriage, which conferred upon women a great benefit. For the Catholic Church, against whose abuses it protested, had taught that marriage was less righteous than celibacy. In its zeal to vindicate the nobleness and rightfulness of marriage Protestantism has demanded that all women shall marry; and until very recently it has invested the position of the unmarried with a certain indefinite contempt. While Catholicism has made it easy for the women who prefer celibacy to live honorably with dignity, and with great usefulness, Protestantism complains of those who, for any reason, fail to be wives and mothers, and reluctantly concedes to them any other career.

Herodotus tells us, that once a year the Babylonians held a wife auction, when all their marriageable girls were disposed of to the highest bidders. The money thus obtained was divided into dowries for the poor and homely girls, whom nobody wanted, but who found purchasers because of the money they carried with them. But all Protestant peoples persist in making marriage the one destiny of women in the face of actual impossibilities, and provide them with no other vocation if, for any cause, wifehood and motherhood fail them. Their custom has been to manufacture, after a fashion, the raw material of girlhood into the stereotype pattern of "good wives;" and then, if there was no market for them, to lay them on the shelf to decay or corrode, or to meet any other fate that might betide.

While other religions have made unmarried women their priestesses no proposition is received to-day with greater disfavor than that women shall be inducted into the ministry of the Christian religion. It is universally admitted that women are more religious than men. Three-fifths of the communicants in Protestant churches, as well as the majority of worshippers in Protestant congregations, are women. When the disciples of Christ forsook him and fled, women pressed through the brutal, murderous throng to the foot of the cross, and remained to the terrible end. Women would have embalmed his dead body. Women sped through the gray dawn of the morning, and were the first at his sepulchre. It was a woman to whom Christ first revealed himself, and whom he commissioned to preach the tidings of his resurrection. And from that hour to the present women have given to the Christian religion heroic devotion, unselfish consecration, and a service which no ostracism nor persecution has been able to hinder. Why should not devout women of noble lives and large gifts, when duly qualified, be admitted to the ministerial profession, as they are to that of medicine and the law?

MARRIAGE NOT THE ONLY BUSINESS OF WOMEN.

Let me not be understood as depreciating marriage. God forbid! It is one of the most beneficent institutions with which we are endowed. If the sun were what the Greeks fabled he was,— a god riding through the heavens,— he might be pardoned if he halted his chariot at noonday, and retarded his plunge down the slope of the west, to gaze into the beauty of the perfect home made by the perfect marriage. But notwithstanding my exalted conception of marriage, and the tendency that grows within me with increasing years to see a spiritual law underlying it, of which I knew nothing in my earlier life, I yet utterly object to the theory that the only legitimate business of women is marriage; or, as Dr.

Maudsley expresses it, that "the woman who misses marriage misses every thing." Immediately, on reading this wholesale assertion, there rise up visions of hosts of women who *in* marriage have "missed every thing." What then?

Equally monstrous is the assertion of Dr. E. H. Clarke, who, in "Sex in Education," declares that "the problem of woman's sphere is not to be solved by applying to it abstract principles of right and wrong. Its solution must be obtained from physiology, not from ethics or metaphysics. The question must be submitted to Agassiz and Huxley; not to Kant or Calvin, to Church or Pope." If women were the possessors of bodies only, there might be some foundation for this amazing statement; but, as they have mental and moral natures as well as physical, their sphere can no more be determined by physiology than that of men. The spheres of both men and women are to be defined by their tastes and their capacities, as well as by their physiology. All that they are in themselves should enter into the settlement of the problem, as well as their various environments. No *doctrinaire*, no physiologist, no church, and no pope can propound an arbitrary theory concerning the sphere of women which it is worth while for women to aim to realize. For there is no Procrustean bed of correct length on which to measure them, drawing them out, or cutting them off, as they are too long or too short. Above the titles of wife and mother, which, although dear, are transitory and accidental, there is the title of human being, which precedes and out-ranks every other. Womanhood comes in advance of wifehood and motherhood, and rises above it, as manhood is more than husbandhood or fatherhood; and the woman who lives up to a noble ideal of womanhood cannot make her life a failure, albeit she may be no man's wife, and no child's mother.

Let it be granted, that in an ideal state every man will have a wife, and every woman a husband; that the husband will be the bread-winner, and the wife the bread-maker; that the work of the man will be to obtain the livelihood, and that of the woman to make the home. We are far enough from an ideal state at present; and, while working up to it, it is wisdom to provide for the necessities that press upon us to-day. Woman was made for man, as man for woman, — no more and no less. But both are to live for God and humanity. When they unite in marriage they have equal rights and mutual responsibilities; and while living for each other they are to tend towards a higher ideal, — that of the Infinite Perfection. No more demoralizing doctrine was ever taught, and none more belittling to woman, than that propounded by Milton in the oft-quoted line, —

"He for God only: she for God in him," —

a doctrine which Eve seems to have accepted; for we soon find her addressing the weak Adam in this fulsome strain, —

"God is thy law; thou, mine: to know no more
Is woman's happiest knowledge and her praise."

The world is outgrowing this ethical nonsense; and women, married and single, are more and more held to a stern accountability for their deeds, words, and influence. And this is as it should be.

Who are the women whom the social scientists insult with the adjective "superfluous," at whom misogynists sneer as "old maids," and whom sociologists brand as "social failures"? A glance at them reveals the fact, that in many instances they are the most useful women in society. Were they expatriated to-morrow the resultant misery to many classes — notwithstanding the good work wrought by modern institutions — would be almost as great as that which followed the immediate dissolution of the monasteries in the time of the Reformation.

CATHOLIC "SUPERFLUOUS WOMEN."

As early as the year 385 Paula, a noble Roman lady, a lineal descendant of the Scipios and Gracchi, and a Christian woman of remarkable benevolence, gathered the remains of her large fortune, which had been expended in charities in the city of Rome, still a pagan city, and sailed for Palestine. Her friend Fabiola had founded a hospital at Rome; and St. Jerome, also her friend, had established another in "Bethlehem of Judea." Paula assembled a community of women about her, who, with herself, consecrated themselves to good works, and deeds of charity. She built several hospitals on roads leading to Bethlehem. For, as there was then no medical staff attached to armies, no sanitary nor Christian commission, no hospitals, and no organized societies of the "Red Cross," such as exist to-day in thirty-two nations, the condition of men wounded in battle was deplorable. When they fell, they were left to die on the field; or, endeavoring to find their way to the nearest hamlet, they dropped by the roadside, — jackals and dogs rending their flesh while they yet lived, and birds of prey picking out their sad eyes before death closed them. From the moment that Paula began her work communities of charitable women multiplied. They renounced marriage, and devoted themselves to charity and piety. This may be said to have been the beginning of the conventual system. It was a holy beginning. Santa Paula, — for she was afterwards canonized by the church, — with her corps of assistants, was the predecessor of Florence Nightingale, and her trained nurses, who, fifteen hundred years later, gave themselves to hospital service in the Crimea Of the former an old historian writes, —

"She was marvellous debonaire and piteous to them that were sicke, and comforted them, and served them right humbly, and gave them largely to eat, such as they asked. But to herself she was hard in her sickness and scarce, for she refused to eat flesh, how well she gave it to others, and also to drink wine. She was oft by them that were sicke, and she laid the pillows aright, and in point, and she rubbed their feet, and boiled water to wash them. And it seemed to her that the lesse she did to the sicke in service, so much the lesse service did she to God, and deserved the lesse mercy. Therefore she was to them piteous, and nothing to herself."

The ancients took but little care of the sick and infirm; and the *hospitalia* of the Romans were for the accommodation of guests, and not for invalids. When, therefore, Christian converts were seized with a divine mania for founding hospitals, and for ministering to the poor and diseased, they had an unoccupied field before them. The enthusiasm ran like prairie-fire. Women of wealth gave all their property for these asylums of the unfortunate and the utterly miserable; and high-born maidens eagerly took the vow of life-long celibacy with a joy not evinced by those who were given away in marriage. It was the genius of Christianity that inspired them, — the impulse that is born of unselfish love, the outcome of a higher type of religion. Hospitals increased; a notable one being built at Cæsarea in the fourth century, and another by Chrysostom at Constantinople. And wherever there was a demand for these celibate women nurses they responded gladly to the summons.

In the seventh century the Bishop of Paris founded a hospital, since known as "Hotel Dieu," as a general refuge for disease and misery, and placed it under the direction of the "Hospitalières," or nursing sisters of the time, whose services were voluntary, and were given from motives of piety. They also had renounced marriage, and buried, in a grave so deep that they could know no resurrection, the dearest earthly hopes that women know. Pope Innocent IV. united these sisters under the rule of the Augustine Order, and made them amenable to the government of the church. To this day the "Hotel Dieu" with its thousand beds, the "Hospital of St. Louis" with seven hundred, and that of "La Pitié" with six hundred more, are served by this same sisterhood of Hospitalières, under whose care they were originally placed centuries ago.

Then came the "Sisters of Charity," formerly called "Gray Sisters" on account of the color of their dress, — independent associations of unmarried women, among whom have been produced some of the most perfect types of women in Christendom. They visited the sick in their homes, and also in hospitals, ministered to the poor, and sought to alleviate human misery wherever they found it, and whatever might be its cause. Howard the philanthropist speaks of this order in terms of glowing eulogy, because of their tender, efficient, and excellent methods in nursing the sick. In 1685 this society had already numbered two hundred and twenty-four convents. The French Revolution sorely interrupted the abundant and benevolent labors of these sisters; but their unwearied charity and devotion had made them so useful to all classes that the merciless Revolution spared them. They continued their work of beneficence secretly, but without restraint. One of the first acts of the new French government was to restore them; and a field of usefulness was opened to them by Napoleon, who placed them under the protection of his mother, and granted them the necessary funds for their work. There exist at present more than three hundred of these associations in France, where, in the villages, elementary education is in great part conducted by them. They attend the sick in all the great hospitals; and in times of epidemics, or when pestilence rages, they become veritable angels to the sick poor, knowing no fear, braving every danger, and often dying at their post.

Then came the Ursuline Sisters, who chose for their vocation the care and instruction of poor children. Long before Protestants entered into this work they had established infant and ragged schools. A community to take charge of children, to teach, to train teachers, and to fit them for their work, was not known in Christendom until 1537, when the Order of the Ursuline Sisters was instituted. So great was the intellectual contempt in which women were held at that time, and so absurd seemed any movement to organize a systematic education for their own sex, that, when Françoise de Saintonges undertook to found a girls' school at Dijon, she was hooted in the streets. Her father called together four doctors of the law to decide on his daughter's mania for educating girls, which came, as he declared, from her possession by the devil. And when at last her earnestness overcame his opposition he dared not openly countenance her; and she began her first community of Ursulines in a garret, unaided, with five poor children. Twelve years later she was carried in triumph through the streets of Dijon, bells ringing, and flowers strewed in her path. She had succeeded, and the church had taken her under its wing.

The Sisters of St. Martha were bound by a religious obligation to active secular duties.

"Les Crêches" was the name of another sisterhood, which took charge of the infant children of poor women compelled to go out from their homes for work. The Order of the Good Shepherd sought the reformation of fallen women, and established houses for them, where they were re-instated in virtuous ways of living, and taught self-supporting industries. The Sisters of Mercy visited the sick and prisoners, instructed poor girls, protected virtuous women in distress, and founded "houses of mercy," where destitute women of good character were cared for until employment was given them.

In short every department of the world's work and woe, every phase of its sorrow and sin, every stage of its weakness and weariness, has been invaded by these consecrated sisterhoods of the Catholic Church. For fifteen hundred years they have glorified the world by the lustre of their lives. They renounced wifehood that they might become the helpers of all men and women; they denied themselves motherhood that all children might be enfolded in their motherly arms. And, if there have been dark pages in their history, we must remember that they have lived in the darkest ages of the past, and are to be judged by the standard of their time, and not by that of to-day. Even in the periods when the convents were most debased, when moral degradation pressed most deeply on them and on the surrounding nations, they undoubtedly helped more than they hindered, — illumined, rather than added to the darkness.

For when the solid earth shook under the tramp of armies they were sent to the field of battle to minister to the wounded. When towns were beleaguered by cordons of besieging camps hostilities were suspended, that these defenceless women might pass within to take charge of the military hospitals. When plague mowed down the panic-stricken people till there were none to bury the dead their courage proved a tonic to the sick, and their ministrations soothed the anguish of the dying. Into the prison-infirmaries, where the branded and condemned felons lay cursing and writhing in despair, they entered with angelic presence. They nursed the wretched criminals perishing with disease; and, as they convalesced, read to them, taught them to read, to knit, and even to sing. They calmed the frenzy of the insane, who ceased to blaspheme, and were unchained and clothed; received homeless orphans to the welcome of their motherly bosoms, and gave to unsheltered weakness the sanctuary of their protection. To whole generations they have been the only exponents of the divine compassion; and it was in large part due to them that faith in the Infinite Goodness did not die out utterly during the semi-barbaric ages of European history.

I am neither a Catholic, nor an advocate of the monastic institutions of that church. Similar organizations established on the basis of the Protestant religion, and in harmony with republican principles, might be made very helpful to modern society, and would furnish occupation and give position to large numbers of unmarried women, whose hearts go out to the world in charitable intent. But I can never forget my experience during the War of the Rebellion. Never did I meet these Catholic sisters in hospitals, on transports, or hospital-steamers, without observing their devotion, faithfulness, and unobtrusiveness. They gave themselves no airs of superiority or holiness, shirked no duty, sought no easy place, bred no mischiefs. Sick and wounded men watched for their entrance into the wards at morning, and looked a regretful farewell when they departed at night. They broke down in exhaustion from overwork, as did the Protestant nurses: like them, they succumbed to the fatal prison-fever, which our exchanged prisoners brought from the fearful pens of the South.

My home was in Chicago years ago, when its condition was most unsanitary, and its unpaved, unsewered streets gave no promise of their present improvements. Cholera, slowly tracking its way westward from the seaboard, like a sleuth-hound, appeared in the city. The death-rate ran up rapidly day after day; and panic seized the people. All who could fled to the country; and every outgoing railroad-train and steamer were loaded with the fugitives. Panic-stricken with the rest I besought my husband, with weak, cowardly tears, to seek for our little children and ourselves a refuge from the pestilence. He was a clergyman, and duty compelled him to remain; nor could I change his purpose. He would seek a place of safety for his family, but they must go without him. That was not to be thought of. Oppressed with vague, indefinite terror, with which it is impossible to reason, and which will not be quelled, I decided to remain also, but to acquaint myself with the dreaded plague, — to know what were its manifestations, what its preventives, and what its remedies.

Early the next morning I found my way to that part of the city where, amid poverty, ignorance, and filth, death was reaping mighty harvests. Dead-carts were clattering through the streets. From one house they gathered two, from another three; from yet another, the entire family. Shops were closed; and people refused to their nearest neighbors the commonest services of friendliness if cholera had made its appearance among them. Amid the squalor, the terror, the despair, the sickness and death of the ignorant people, mainly of foreign birth, the Sisters of Charity and Mercy moved like angels of healing. To some they administered remedies; to others they spoke in calm and assured tones, soothing their fright. They took in charge the orphaned children, rebuked the cowardly selfishness that stood aloof from the sufferers, and encouraged with divine hope the dying.

"Have you no fear of cholera?" I inquired of one, who was endeavoring to arouse courage in a man, whose wife and child had just been taken out to the dead-cart, and who was writhing in abject fear. "Do you not regard it contagious?"

"Until the hour comes appointed me to die, I am immortal!" was her answer; "and, if one must die, is there a nobler place than the post of duty?" I felt the tonic of her reply immediately, and gladly listened to her directions. And as it became apparent to me that the pestilence was largely preventable, and that it had a manageable stage, as I witnessed her fearlessness in its presence, and her skilful administration of remedies, the burden rolled from my heart, and my fear was gone forever. Dismissing me with a small package of the remedies she employed, and with written prescriptions for others, she said, "Whatsoever else you do, do not yield to fear; for we could soon banish the cholera from this quarter if we could halt the panic of these poor people."

Not even when cholera invaded their own ranks, and two of their number succumbed to the swift disease, did they falter in their work. Not a Protestant nurse aided them; for there were but few of these in the entire city, and none who were trained, nor was there an organization to assume the charge of their training. The Sisters of Charity answered the call of any, no matter what their creed. With such memories I should be a narrow bigot indeed, if, because their religious belief is other than mine, I failed to do homage to this noble order of women, who have glorified the last fifteen centuries. These women, by the nomenclature of social science, are "superfluous women," because they are unmarried. Shall we talk such nonsense?

PROTESTANT "SUPERFLUOUS WOMEN."

What shall be said of the "superfluous women" of Protestantism, a great host of whom have come to the front during the last half-century? Who, among the elder women of the day, can forget the delight with which they pored over Maria Edgeworth's novels, all aglow with humane sympathies, and the highest moral tendencies? — or the sketches and reminiscences of Miss Mitford, with their cheerful tone of kindness and domesticity, their mingled humor and pathos, their simple but finished style; or the more serious moral and religious works of Hannah More, which, forty years ago, were found in the bookcase of every well-regulated young woman; or the dramas of Joanna Baillie, in each of which it was her aim, as it was that of Miss Edgeworth in her novels, to elucidate one particular passion or vice.

The whole civilized world has been brought

into debt to Harriet Martineau, whose life of seventy-four years was one of untiring industry, and immense accomplishment. Not a question of moment to the race ever found her apathetic to its claims, and in her treatment of them she was often in advance of her age. Whether the question was one of political economy, education, government, labor and land reform, social purity, the rights of women, anti-slavery, peace, religious belief, temperance, or hygiene, she immediately identified herself with it, accepting uncomplainingly all the reproach and ostracism such identification was sure to bring. At her death she had published one hundred and seven volumes, all of the utmost practical importance at the moment, and many of them dealing with problems which will reach far into coming time. If her magazine and fugitive articles of moment had been republished in book form, as her friends desired, the number of her volumes would have been increased to one hundred and seventy-five or two hundred.

Without entering into theories of prison reform, or even understanding them, Sarah Martin, an English philanthropist, fifty years ago, put in practice those which are to-day recommended by the most eminent authorities. She mitigated the horrors of imprisonment, which were inexpressible at that time; provided employment and education for prisoners, superintending both, —

"Fighting her way — the way that angels fight —
With powers of darkness to let in the light."

Angela Burdett Coutts inherited at twenty-three a property estimated at nearly fifteen millions of dollars. Her unmarried life of nearly forty years was devoted to philanthropy, and she sometimes spent her entire yearly income in charities. She built and endowed several churches and schools in England; endowed bishoprics at Cape Town, in Australia and British Columbia; founded an establishment in Australia for the improvement of the aborigines; gave to the city of London the market at Bethnal Green, that the poor of that district might be supplied with good and wholesome food; built Columbia Square, consisting of model dwellings at low rents for three hundred families; established a shelter and reformatory for fallen women; effected reforms in the teaching of girls in the national schools; became a patroness of emigration, assisting poor families in their outfit and passage; educated hundreds of young girls, and provided for their start in life, whether they married or remained single; identified herself with the English Society to prevent Cruelty to Animals; and all the while gave to private charities on a corresponding scale, and patronized art as liberally as if it were her sole interest.

Mary Carpenter was publicly and inseparably connected with the cause of prison reform in England for forty years. Her interest was aroused in neglected children and youthful criminals, to whose unwise treatment she awakened public attention. She founded several reformatories for girls, one of which she personally superintended, and, in the prosecution of her work, visited India three times.

Fredrika Bremer, the Swedish authoress, in her early life endured great suffering and privation, out of which blossomed power and helpfulness for her sex. The series of exquisite novels which she wrote forty years ago opened the Musical Academy of Stockholm to Swedish women, as also its Industrial College, and its Academy of Fine Arts. Not content, she wrote "Hertha," aimed at the tyrannous laws of Sweden concerning women. It so moved King Oscar, that, at the opening of the Swedish Diet, he proposed a bill, granting to women twenty-five years old the control of their property, and if unmarried, and worth four hundred rix-dollars per annum, the right of suffrage.

Rosa Bonheur has achieved world-wide fame and pecuniary independence as one of the most skilful painters of animals; the boldness and independence of her own character inspiring her pencil, and her faithfulness to nature giving great force to her work. The whole civilized world does homage to her genius; and, during the siege of Paris in the Franco-Prussian War, the Crown-Prince of Prussia gave orders that her studio and residence at Fontainebleau should be spared and respected.

Florence Nightingale, well born, highly educated, and brilliantly accomplished, gave herself to the study of hospitals, and of institutions for the diseased, helpless, and infirm. Appreciating the work of the Sisters of Charity in the Catholic church, she felt the need of an institution which should be its counterpart in the Protestant communion. She visited civil and military hospitals all over Europe, studied with the Sisters of Charity in Paris their system of nursing and hospital-management, and went into training as a nurse in the House of the Protestant Deaconesses at Kaiserwerth on the Rhine. For ten years she served an apprenticeship, preparing for the great work of her life. Her opportunity came during the war in the Crimea, when through incompetence, and utter disregard of sanitary laws, the rate of mortality in the English hospitals surpassed that of the fiercest battles. Horror and indignation were felt throughout England. Miss Nightingale offered her services to the government with a corps of trained nurses, was accepted, and went to Constantinople.

The disorder, the want, — while storehouses were bursting with the needed hospital-supplies, — the incompetence, the uncleanliness, the suffering and death, created general dismay. Unappalled by the shocking chaos, Miss Nightingale ordered the storehouses at Scutari to be broken open, when want gave place to abundance; and soon her executive skill and rare knowledge transformed the hospitals into models of order and comfort. She spared herself no labor, sometimes standing twenty hours in succession giving directions, and refusing to leave her post, even when she broke down with hospital-fever. Sadly overworked, her patience and cheerfulness were unfailing, winning the love of the roughest soldiers; and, as she walked the wards, men too weak to speak plucked her gown with feeble fingers, or kissed her shadow as it fell athwart their pillow. She expended her own vitality in this work, and returned to England an invalid for life. But not an idle invalid, for from her sick-room there have gone plans for the improvement of hospitals and the training of nurses wrought out by her busy brain and pen.

Caroline Herschel, sister of the great astronomer, was his constant helper and faithful assistant, in this character receiving a salary from the king. In addition she found time to make her own independent observations, discovering comets, remarkable nebulæ, and clusters of stars, and receiving from the Royal Society a gold medal in recognition of her work.

Charlotte Brontë's portion in life was pain and toil and sorrow. Her experience was a long struggle with every unkindness of fate, and she lacked every advantage supposed necessary to literary work. Her force of character and undismayed persistence triumphed over all hinderances. She put heart and conscience into books that held the literary world in fascination. In them she rent the shams of society by her keen analyses. She depicted life as she had known it, shorn of every illusion, and then beautified it by unflinching loyalty to duty, and unwavering fidelity to conscience. The publication of "Jane Eyre" marked an era in the literary world not soon to be forgotten.

Frances Power Cobbe is the most eminent literary woman of England, whose pen illumines all subjects of which it treats, and who has pursued religious studies with profound interest. Her scholarship, her talent, and her reputation are generously put to the service of women, whom she has recently laid under deep obligations by her incomparable work on "The Duties of Woman."

The Deaconesses of Kaiserwerth, a Protestant sisterhood, are unmarried, although they take no vows of celibacy. They have in charge insane and orphan asylums, infant-schools, and nurses' training-schools, and have established hospitals in Germany, London, Constantinople, Jerusalem, Egypt, Smyrna, and Pittsburg in the United States.

Maria S. Rye has crossed the Atlantic fifteen times, bringing with her, and finding homes and occupations for, twelve hundred poor English girls in British America. She has made three voyages to Australia and New Zealand, finding homes and employment for fifteen hundred more.

Annie MacPherson has crossed the Atlantic ten times, taking with her no fewer than eighteen hundred of the wild street-Arabs of East London. These she has placed in respectable families in Canada, and has established an agency of unpaid co-operators, who watch that the children are well taken care of.

Dorothea Dix, an American philanthropist, has devoted her life to improving the condition of paupers, lunatics, and prisoners. She has suggested reforms, and corrected abuses, and has induced several of the States to found insane-asylums of an improved order. During the war she added to her labors the superintendence of nurses in the hospitals of the Eastern States, and only ceased her labors when advanced years compelled her.

Dr. Elizabeth Blackwell went through the country like a mendicant, knocking at the doors of medical colleges for admission, until that at Geneva, N.Y., was opened to her. Completing her studies in Paris and London, she returned to America to the practice of her profession; establishing, with her sister, Dr. Emily Blackwell, a medical school and infirmary for women in the city of New York, and becoming the noble helper of all worthy women seeking medical training.

Dr. Zakrzewska's early struggles for medical education and position were protracted and severe. Crowned with complete success, her medical skill and noble character make her a tower of strength in the city of Boston, have allayed prejudices against women physicians, and made it easier for all who wish to enter the profession.

Charlotte Cushman's early history was one of privation, and of battling against great odds. But she triumphed, and for forty years walked the paths of a profession dangerous to woman, its most eminent artist, and never by word or deed brought a blush to the cheek of the most fastidious.

Harriet Hosmer, an American sculptor, in her studio at Rome has modelled statuary that the world pauses to admire. Never has her art occupied itself with an unpoetic or unworthy subject: hardly has it descended to mere prettiness even. A lofty thought is visible in all her work; and the moral sense is addressed, no less than the love of art and beauty.

Maria Mitchell, wearing the gold medal of the King of Denmark, for her discovery of a telescopic comet, makes in her observatory, and with her own telescope, observations used by the United-States Government in its coast survey, and in the compilation of the nautical almanac it authorizes. As professor of astronomy at Vassar College she is the inspiration of many of the noblest young women of the time, through whom, as teachers, authors, wives, and mothers, Miss Mitchell's love of truth and scientific pursuit is being perpetuated.

Anne Whitney, a poet gifted with exceptional poetic instinct beyond most writers of modern times; a sculptor whose work takes rank with that of artists at home and abroad, who have won world-wide reputation from their skill in evoking life and beauty from the shapeless marble, — works diligently in her Boston studio, which is peopled with "the beings of her mind." Her sympathy with what is noblest in human character, and loftiest in human deeds, is expressed in her work; and her statues compel admiration by the ideas expressed in them, before one observes the skill with which they are wrought. The heroism, spirit, and dignity of her bronze Samuel Adams, which glorifies Dock Square in Boston, the city of her residence, is felt by thousands who daily pass and repass it, but who would be unable to express their thought in language.

Catherine Beecher consoled herself for the great sorrow of her life by earnest, lifelong work for women. She made it her business to advance their physical, intellectual, and practical education, and organized societies and schools for training teachers, and sending them to the West, where the work of systematic, thorough training was then unbegun.

Mary Lyon also gave herself to the advancement of woman's education, adopting the principles, as motives to progress, which, later, were successfully employed by Dr. Arnold at Rugby. The schools which she founded still live, famed for thoroughness of scholarship, systematic habits, and earnest benevolence.

Susan Dimock's brief and beautiful life as the physician of the Boston Woman's Hospital was radiant with promise of future helpfulness to women. But she went down in the ill-fated "Schiller," that was swallowed by the hungry waves that rage and roar around the Isles of Scilly.

Clara Barton, the first woman to hold an independent clerkship under our government, resigned her office at the breaking out of the war, and devoted herself to the care of wounded soldiers. For four years she endured incredible exposures, sometimes on the field of battle, sometimes at the rear, caring alike for men who wore the blue or the gray if they were wounded. At the close of the war the hell of Andersonville horrors was opened, where thirteen thousand of our brave soldiers had been starved into lunacy, idiocy, and death, and buried in unknown graves. Through her exertions these were identified and marked; Congress reimbursing her, as she had spent her patrimony in this service. Failing in health she went abroad for rest and recuperation, when the Franco-Prussian war broke out; and her services were again in demand for men wounded in battle. She remained until that war was ended, and those hospitals emptied, when she returned to America, to advance the interests of the "Red Cross," a great international humanitarian movement. Meanwhile she is superintendent of the Woman's State Prison in Massachusetts.

Cordelia Green graduated in the same class with the eminent Dr. Zakrzewska of Boston, and has been active since then in the practice of her profession while doing much other noble philanthropic work. Years ago she founded a sanitarium in Western New York, where hundreds of valuable professional women — teachers, returned missionaries, authors, journalists, as well as wives and mothers — have been lifted from invalidism into a new life of health and strength.

Elizabeth Peabody, standing outside of wifehood and motherhood, has developed so wide an interest in kindergarten instruction, that she may be regarded as the mother of all children. Her influence has been extended to the remotest parts of the country; and her labors still continue, although her advanced age would excuse her from active service.

Anna Dickinson, the peerless girl orator, came to the help of the country when its life was imperilled, like a second Joan of Arc. While the nation agonized in a long four-years' struggle with treason, she put her matchless gifts to its service; never faltering in her devotion, but continuing unwearied in her utterances for the right, until the bells rang in the proclamation of peace, and the emancipation of four million of slaves.

To continue the catalogue is to include the names of many of the most eminent women of the day. It will include the name of Louisa Alcott, a blessed providence to the fatherless and motherless children of her own sisters, a tender daughter to the aged mother whose steps she guided down the dark valley, and to the invalid father lingering at the end of life's journey; and who has yet found time and heart to write books for the young, which are caught up and eagerly devoured as fast as the steam-worked press can send them forth.

It cannot omit the name of Elizabeth Stuart Phelps, who in a lifelong struggle with pain, feebleness, and sorrow, and the isolation these compel, has steadily wielded a vigorous pen for the weak against the strong, for the oppressed against the oppressor, for the right against the wrong. She has rendered valiant service to women in many departments of literature, and, from the retiracy of her invalidism, sends them constant sympathy in their long struggle for justice and opportunity.

It holds tenderly the memory of Alice and Phœbe Cary, the gifted daughters of song, who, buffeted by unkind fate, lost fortune, friends, and health, while toil, sorrow, and pain were their sad and steadfast companions. They gave utterance to no weakness of complaint, but in their darkest moments sang, —

> "Like the bird, that, halting in its flight
> A while, on boughs too slight,
> Feels them give way beneath it, and yet sings,
> Knowing that it has wings."

It enrolls on its list of honor the names of Abby May, foremost in the work of the Sanitary Commission a score of years ago, prominent in the work of education and reform to-day; Frances Willard, who has turned from her chosen work of instruction, for which she was carefully fitted, to lead her countrywomen in their righteous hostility to the dram-shop and saloon; Susan B. Anthony, who, graduating from her father's factory, has given herself for thirty years to a fearless advocacy of the rights of woman, receiving therefor unmeasured abuse, bitter calumny, and stinging insult; Lucy Larcom, the sweetness of whose song has cheered many a weary pilgrim on the dusty highways of life; Lucretia Crocker, Ellen Hyde, and Anna Brackett, types of a noble army of women teachers; Susan Hale and Sara Clarke, representatives of an increasing class of women artists, — the latter, the only pupil Washington Allston ever had; Christine Ladd of Johns Hopkins University, one of the ablest writers on mathematics; and Grace

Anna Lewis, a devotee of science, whose influence upon women is to lead them away from the cultivation of worthless accomplishments, towards higher pursuits.

To continue this catalogue would be to enumerate most of the American women of the last quarter of a century who have been known to the public through rare worth, or the achievements of their lives. They have failed to realize the generally accepted theory of woman's being, and, as they have not married, are swept by the classification of the day into the category of "superfluous women" and "social failures." But, bereft of them, the world would suffer heavy loss, and society be halted in its noblest endeavors. For they have been foremost in deeds of philanthropy and self-sacrifice; they have given new power to literature and art; they have borne the benignity of their presence, and the helpfulness of their strong souls, into hospitals and prisons; they have carried healing and comfort to battle-fields, overhung with the sulphurous smoke of gunpowder, and burdened with the tainted atmosphere of blood. On every round of the ladder of learning they stand to-day, from the lowest to the highest, like the angels of the patriarch's dream, lifting the sons and daughters of this generation to a higher intellectual level than their parents ever knew.

Trained and educated as physicians and surgeons, they have entered the lists against the many ills to which flesh is heir, and are routing the appalling physical ailments which have threatened to make womanhood interchangeable with invalidism. In the church, they are the priestesses of religion, repeating the lessons of love, patience, and self-abnegation, which God and life have taught them. In asylums, with the gentleness of compassion, they are as mothers to hapless children, orphaned by poverty, crime, or death. In reformatories, they are ingenious in devising methods for the exorcism of the spirit of evil from the poor women in their charge, and patient in their efforts to win them to nobler ways of life than they have hitherto known. In the South, they are the consecrated educators of the freedmen, battling with the colossal vice and ignorance which two centuries of slavery have entailed on their slow pupils. To India, to China, to Mexico, they carry civilization, teach domestic virtue and industry, shelter the outcast and the friendless; and, surrounded by swarthy students, they unfold to them the mysteries of their own physiology, the art of healing, and the science of medicine, that these may, in their turn, become physicians and nurses to their own sex. To paragraph their names and deeds, is to rehearse a fragment of the roll-call of God's saints, to whom he will open wide the doors of his heaven with the plaudit, " Well done, ye good and faithful ! "

All through the highways and byways of life, there are other women of whom the world takes small account, disparaging them as " old maids," — employing the vulgar parlance of every-day speech with a shrug of the shoulder and a dash of scorn. They have been brave enough to choose to walk through life alone, rather than accept a husband to whom their hearts refused allegiance; or, with white lips, they have said " No," while love has prompted a different response, because duty has demanded of them the sacrifice of their individual happiness; or they remain faithful to a grave, and plant no second flower of love to bloom above it. They make of their lives stepping-stones for the advancement of younger sisters. They earn the money that pays the expenses of brothers through colleges into professions. They uphold the roof-tree over a dependent household, like the caryatides of architecture. They invert the order of nature, and become mothers to aged parents, whom they lead gently down the hill of life, folding their hands, and pillowing their heads in the peaceful slumber that knows no waking. They carry comfort, strength, and cheer to homes invaded by trouble, crime, sorrow, sickness, and death. The care of an invalid brother or sister, of a maniac, a dissolute or an imbecile member of their kindred, brings early pallor to their cheek, and premature frosts to their thinning hair. They merge their very identity in those whom they love, and for whom they live.

The dusty years stretch far behind them. Beauty and comeliness drop away from them, and they grow faded and worn before their time. They become nobodies to the hurrying, rushing, bustling world, which leaves them in lonely isolation. By and by they will slip out into the gloom, — the shadows will veil them forever from earthly vision ; and then, as they pass through the low gateway that we call death, into "that other chamber of the King, larger than this, and lovelier," the great surprise of a joyful welcome will reveal to them the noble quality of their uncrowned heroism.

Stewart, with palatial stores filled with costly fabrics, — a fortune of one hundred millions, — gave one million from his superabundance for the building of a cheap hotel for working-women, which proved a failure; and the world echoed the praise of his generosity. Peabody, from his princely wealth, gave libraries and institutes to towns in the North, and educational funds to the South; and the glory of great beneficence will gild his memory forever. Vanderbilt and Drew put millions to the service of institutions of learning, which will transmit their names to the future, as generous patrons of higher education. But these unknown, unsung heroines have made larger individual gifts than either of these munificent donors. For they gave but a pittance from easily-won fortunes, colossal in their magnitude; and these poor women give their all, — *themselves*, with a wealth of unlimited devotion, with their possibilities of happiness, their dreams of the future.

Not so heroic was the march of three-starred Grant and Sherman, through the bristling Wilderness, or from Atlanta to the sea, as is the lonely passage through life made by many an unmated woman, of whom the world knows nothing, save as her celibate life serves to point a jest, or add piquancy to a story. For they were stimulated by the cheers and prayers of a nation; and the world looked on with admiring gaze, and held its breath, wondering what the end would be. But the solitary path of these women leads them afar from companionship, and often from congenial pursuits. Instead of receiving the stimulus of approval and sympathy, they are not unfrequently met with ingratitude and non-appreciation. They are pelted with the hot shot of ridicule, riddled with the arrows of satire, or stung with a contemptuous and patronizing pity.

### WHO ARE "SUPERFLUOUS WOMEN"?

Superfluous women! There are plenty of them, and of superfluous men also, who might drop out by the ten thousand during a night, and the world would not know at the breakfast-hour that it had lost any thing. Nor would it lose any thing, save a minimum of the weight on its back, or of the drag on its wheels. But you will not always find superfluous women among the unmarried. *They* are superfluous women, whether married or unmarried, whose lives are days of idle pleasure, and who are victims of *ennui*, unrest, and morbid fancy, because they despise the activities of the age into which they are born.  Truly has Elizabeth Barrett Browning said,—

> "The honest, earnest man must stand and work;
> The woman also — otherwise she drops
> At once below the dignity of man,
> Accepting serfdom."

The world has no need of women who feel themselves degraded to the level of servitude when compelled to engage in practical work.

They are superfluous women, who, with imbecile renunciation, hasten to wash their reputations of the taint of "strong-mindedness;" whose intellects are "accidents of the body," and, "like the candles inside Chinese lanterns, are of use only to light up, and show off to advantage, the pretty devices outside." They are superfluous women, who are so indifferent to duty, so lacking in high principle, so devoid of tender feeling, that they are capable of accepting any man in marriage — an octogenarian, an imbecile, a debauchee — if his establishment, his equipage, and bank-account are satisfactory; these being of more value than the man who offers them, and whose adjuncts they are. They are superfluous women, who, anchored in the haven of a husband's love, and surrounded by the severely earned luxury of his toil, are steeped in selfishness, rebelling against motherhood, scouting philanthropy, and answering the plea of their less fortunate sisters with the shameful iteration, "I will not be disturbed! I have all the rights I want!" They are superfluous women, who live for what they call "society," their weak natures knowing no loftier aspiration than to be admitted to a gilded social circle higher than they; whose whole duty is comprised in swift obedience to the dictates of folly and fashion; to whom the tittle-tattle of gossip is as the nectar of the gods, and whose instinct for scandal and intrigue is as keen as the scent of the vulture for the battle when it rages.

It is the false teaching of society — a demoralizing public sentiment — that is responsible for these women. As long as women are taught to believe that a life of ease is better than work; that they are born into the world to be the dependents of men, whose inferiors they are; that it is their mission to please and amuse men, and not to stimulate them to high endeavor; as long as courage and capacity, self-poise and independence, are regarded as qualities ennobling men, but de-womanizing women, — so long will low ideals of womanhood prevail, necessarily dragging down the standard of manhood. While society in its highways and byways, in its drawing-rooms and workshops, by hints and suggestions, through novels and essays, lectures, sermons, and editorials, in season and out of season, dins in the ears of young women, "Marry! marry! for the unmarried woman fails of the end for which she was created!" we may expect them to rush into marriage without thought or preparation, and to regard it as a man does business or trade. We may also expect that the unmarried woman will be regarded with disfavor, that her position will be considered less honorable than that of the wife; thus perpetuating an estimate of woman that belongs to a rude age, when population was sparse, development low, and the wants of the world were physical.

### RELATION OF MAN AND WOMAN.

Let the estimate of woman be changed, so that she shall be valued for what she is in herself. If she have no value as woman, never can she be valuable as mother. Let her training be changed, so that while she shall retain every grace and charm of the feminine nature, nor lose one attribute of womanliness, she shall have more fibre, firmness, and capacity; so that, whether married or unmarried, she shall have character, ability to stand alone, value in herself, enriching the society of which she forms an integral part. This would be no less helpful to man than to woman. For men and women do not make two classes, but one. The man is the masculine half, the woman the feminine half, each having qualities the other lacks, each the complement and the supplement of the other. Neither the man nor the woman is superior or inferior, but equal and different, and meant to be different.

If the man announce himself the head, I shall certainly not dispute it: he may have it so. But, assuming that he is the head, I shall demand that he be the head. For no greater calamity can befall a woman than when the man with whom her life is associated denies his headship. When he might wield the sceptre and wear the royal purple of an incomparable manhood, for him to discrown himself, and wear instead the rags of a dissolute life, is to dethrone her, and to rob her of her crown. But, if the man be head, what is the woman? All concede, with haste and unanimity, that she is the heart. Which is the more necessary, the head, or the heart? Shall the head set up for itself, that the heart is its inferior in value?

Or shall the heart demand that the head shall yield to its claim of superiority? Are not both of equal value to the body, each vitally important to its existence, while the functions of each are unlike?

Is it claimed that the man is wisdom? I will make no denial, but answer that the woman is love. And what is love? A weak, gushing, effusive quality, that makes the weakness of woman? Nay. Love is rest; it is warmth, comfort, nourishment, strength, home; it is life; it is the omnipotence of very God. As the head has no life till the heart quickens it, so wisdom is not wise till love informs it. Not a manly quality can be mentioned, that is not supplemented by a womanly trait. You cannot exalt man, but woman shall share his elevation: you cannot degrade woman, without also lowering man. We are so indissolubly united, that each must share the lot of the other.

> "We rise or sink together,
> Dwarfed or godlike, bond or free."

We are told of a mythical bird that had but one wing. Neither the male nor the female bird could fly alone. They came together; and then, on the side that was wingless, there was a muscular development, so that they joined forces as we clasp hands. Then one pair of wings sufficed for both. They spurned the ground, they soared above the mists and fogs of earth into the clear ether, and on tireless wing held their way towards the ever-living, ever-shining sun.

That bird is Humanity. Alone, man grovels. Alone, woman does not rise. Alone, man rarely seeks the highest altitude of his being. Alone, woman rarely attains to her largest life. Together — as husband and wife, as brother and sister, as co-worker or friend, commingling as we do in modern society — one noble aim, one high ideal, one divine inspiration, stirs the hearts of both. It takes both away from their low ideals, from their petty theories of life, from dim groping and blind struggling in the dark, into a clearer atmosphere, up to a higher outlook. And then begins the slow but steady flight towards that Infinite Perfection which, on bended knee and with reverent lip, we call God.

"THE GREAT "LAWSUIT," AS MARGARET FULLER CALLED IT."

## Common Sense about Women.

BY THOMAS WENTWORTH HIGGINSON.

16mo. Cloth, $1.50.

"These essays are very short ones, no longer than Addison's, in the *Spectator*, for there are 105 in the space of 400 not very large pages, and they present a great many aspects of the question of sex, and the minor morals of American and English life. Of course they all take the woman's side of the great "Lawsuit," as Margaret Fuller called it, but this is done fairly and without undue assumption or extravagance in declamation. The titles of the chapters are casual, and sometimes too expressive, but the essay will often be found more serious than the title, though wit abounds in the seasoning of this dish of argument and homily."—*Springfield Republican.*

"A thoroughly good and practical book, from the pen and heart of Thomas Wentworth Higginson. If one of its short chapters could be read aloud every day during the year, in the millions of homes in the land, its power for good could scarcely be overestimated."—*Chicago Inter-Ocean.*

"The work is made up of more than a hundred short, bright, breezy essays, exceedingly readable, and well calculated to carry conviction to a candid mind. The author takes a common-sense view of woman's position, and, though he does not spare sarcasm in dealing with those who would deny her equal rights with man, he does not exalt her into an angel, whose participation in politics is to reform the world."—*Portland Transcript.*

"Altogether the book is one of the most practical and strong arguments, based upon fact and common sense, in favor of the equality of women, which we have seen. It is without heat, without rant, but it is cool, strong, to the point, and on the score of justice and right, its arguments are very difficult to successfully refute."—*Bridgeport Standard.*

*⁎* Sold by all booksellers and newsdealers, or sent by mail, postpaid, on receipt of price.

# EUROPEAN BREEZES.
## By MARGERY DEANE.
### Cloth, gilt top, $1.50.

Being chapters of travel through Germany, Austria, Hungary and Switzerland, covering places not usually visited by Americans in making "The grand tour of the Continent," by the accomplished writer of "Newport Breezes." Mrs. Pitman weaves the same charm about the daily European life as she met it, that we find in her delightful "*Newport Breezes*," — the charm of a cultivated lady whose eyes and ears are ready servants, and whose versatile pen is quick to make the record.

"It is a delightful and entertaining volume, giving much important information in a 'breezy,' pleasant way." — *Chronicle-Herald, Philadelphia.*

"Clear, unaffected, direct, and really graphic." — *Sat. Evening Gazette.*

"Breezy and full of life; life as seen and felt by one capable of viewing it and realizing at every step." — *Boston Correspondent Beverly Citizen.*

"Abounds in bright, cheerful scenes that gain the reader's loyal attention at once." — *Sunday Times.*

"A contribution full of bright touches and quotable passages to the higher literature of travel." — *Springfield Republican.*

"Her style is piquant and 'breezy,' and one enjoys what she has to say from the first page to the last." — *Boston Commonwealth.*

"Mrs. Pitman's style has the charm of directness, freshness and enthusiasm, which permits her readers to feel that she is addressing them personally. The book deals with matters one is particularly desirous to know about." — *Boston Herald.*

"Tells entertainingly of her personal experiences in Hungary, where the writer was in some places the first American lady to be introduced into society." — *Philadelphia Evening News.*

*⁎* Sold by all booksellers and newsdealers, or sent by mail, postpaid, on receipt of price.

# HIGGINSON'S WORKS.

### I.
### OUT-DOOR PAPERS. 16mo. $1.50.

"That wise and gracious Bible of physical education." — PROF. M. C. TYLER, *in Brownville Papers.*

"The chapters on 'Water-Lilies,' 'The Life of Birds,' and 'The Procession of Flowers' are charming specimens of a poetic faculty in description, combined with a scientific observation and analysis of nature." — *London Patriot.*

### II.
### MALBONE: AN OLDPORT ROMANCE. 16mo. $1.50.

"As a 'romance' it seems to us the most brilliant that has appeared in this country since Hawthorne (whom the author in some points has the happiness to resemble) laid down the most fascinating pen ever held by an American author." — JOHN G. SAXE.

### III.
### ARMY LIFE IN A BLACK REGIMENT. 16mo. $1.50.

"His narratives of his works and adventures in 'The Atlantic Monthly' attracted general attention by their graphic humor and their picturesque and poetical descriptions." — *London Spectator.*

### IV.
### ATLANTIC ESSAYS. 16mo. $1.50.

"A book which will most assuredly help to raise the standard of American literature. Mr. Higginson's own style is, after Hawthorne's, the best which America has yet produced. He possesses simplicity, directness, and grace. We must strongly recommend this volume of essays, not to be merely read, but to be studied. It is as sound in substance as it is graceful in expression." — *Westminster Review.*

### V.
### OLDPORT DAYS. *With 10 Heliotype Illustrations.* 16mo. $1.50.

"Mr. Higginson's 'Oldport Days' have an indescribable charm. The grace and refinement of his style are exquisite. His stories are pleasant; his pictures of children and his talk about them are almost pathetic in their tenderness; but in his descriptions of nature he is without a rival." — *Boston Daily Advertiser.*

### VI.
### COMMON SENSE ABOUT WOMEN. 16mo. $1.50.

"A thoroughly good and practical book, from the pen and heart of Thomas Wentworth Higginson. If one of its short chapters could be read aloud every day during the year, in the millions of homes in the land, its power for good could scarcely be overestimated." — *Chicago Inter-Ocean.*

**LEE & SHEPARD, Publishers, Boston.**

www.ingramcontent.com/pod-product-compliance
Lightning Source LLC
LaVergne TN
LVHW041616070426
835507LV00008B/278